FUCHSIAS

Fuchsias

The Complete Guide

George Bartlett

The Crowood Press

First published in 1988 by
The Crowood Press Ltd
Ramsbury, Marlborough
Wiltshire SN8 2HR

Paperback edition 1993

British Library Cataloguing in Publication Data

A catalogue record for this book is available from the British Library.

ISBN 1 85223 745 7

Acknowledgements

Photographs by Leslie Hobbs (L.R.P.S.)
Line illustrations by Janet Sparrow

Typeset by Inforum
Rowlands Castle, Hants
Printed in Great Britain
by Redwood Press Ltd, Melksham

Contents

Foreword

From its relative obscurity in the early part of the century, the fuchsia has grown in favour to become one of today's most popular plants. This should come as no surprise to those who know the fuchsia, for it is one of our most versatile plants, and cultivars and species can be grown equally successfully in the greenhouse or the garden. As this book demonstrates, fuchsias can enhance a large garden as much as they can a small window box or city apartment. Here you will find information on all aspects of fuchsia growing, suitable both for the expert and the beginner, written by someone who makes his enthusiasm for the subject evident.

I write as someone who grew up in the years when fuchsias were still something of an obscurity, and certainly there were few books on the subject. When my brother, Revd Dr H.A. Brown, began his specialist collection in the 1930s, he was breaking practically new ground. Things are very different today, and this happy change has largely been brought about by people like George Bartlett who, with untiring dedication, have helped to spread the word.

Those comparatively few of us who have had the great pleasure of hearing the author lecture on this subject have long wished that he would write a book so that his capacity for encouraging others in word and demonstration might reach a wider audience. Now, at last, he has done so. This book will give enormous pleasure to its many readers and will further even more the success of that loveliest of flowers, the fuchsia.

Margaret Slater
Past President of the British Fuchsia Society
Holder of the Whiteman Medal of Honour

Introduction

I have been growing fuchsias since 1966 and have come to greatly admire their beauty and diversity. But why should anyone wish to specialise in the growing of one type of plant? And why choose fuchsias? These are questions which have been asked on numerous occasions and I suppose the answer will always be the same. The fuchsia is so amenable that anyone can grow good plants with a minimum of effort. They are very easy to propagate and they can be used in so many different ways. There is no exact science in the growing of fuchsias – a dozen different 'experts' will advocate a dozen different methods, and each one will ensure success.

Within this book I have endeavoured to describe 'my' way of growing these marvellous plants. Although I have been concerned with the showing of fuchsias, as an exhibitor, an organiser and a judge, I do not want to give the impression that this is primarily a book for prospective showmen. No, I want people to grow fuchsias for the sake of growing fuchsias; to grow them because they like them; and to enjoy growing them. It is important to achieve success with a minimum of effort and I hope I will succeed in encouraging you to seek and find that success. If you then choose to enter the show arena to share your enjoyment with others, I wish you luck and hope that your efforts will do much to enhance the fuchsia 'shop-window', which is of benefit to all.

Growing fuchsias should not be a serious pastime unless you are a totally dedicated showman – it should be enjoyed and you should have fun. Perhaps the title of this book might have been *Have Fun with Fuchsias*!

I am grateful to have been offered the opportunity of sharing my enthusiasm and 'fun' with you.

George Bartlett

1

The History
of the Fuchsia

It is often a source of wonder to many people as to why a plant first discovered in the year 1703 by a missionary and botanist, Father Charles Plumier, should be named after a sixteenth-century botanist and Doctor of Medicine, Leonhard Fuchs. The reasoning behind the choice of name will probably never be known, but there is no doubt that Plumier held a great admiration and respect for Fuchs. We do know, however, that Father Charles Plumier first described *Fuchsia tryphilla, flore coccinea* which he had discovered in the Dominican Republic.

For the next eighty-five years little is known of the fuchsia although it is possible that fresh discoveries were being made. In 1788, just two hundred years ago, a Captain Firth presented a fuchsia plant to Kew Gardens and at that time it was referred to as *F. coccinea*. At about the same time, it is believed, James Lee, a nurseryman from Hammersmith, acquired a plant of similar type and started to produce many new plants from it. The fascinating tale explains how Lee managed to persuade a lady, who lived in Wapping, to part with an unusual plant which had been seen growing in her window. The plant was extremely attractive, with flowers hanging pendulously from arching branches, of a type completely unknown to James Lee. A sum of money, a fortune for those days, apparently changed hands and it was not long before Lee, using his skill as a nurseryman, had multiplied the number of plants by three hundred and managed to sell them for a very handsome profit.

Time in the development and discovery of plants passes quite quickly, and by the year 1844 many new species had been discovered and recorded in various parts of the world:

1796	*F lycioides*	1840	*F. corymbiflora*
1824	*F. arborescens*	1843/44	*F. apetala, F. decussata, F. serratifolia*
1827	*F. magellanica*		*F. dependens*
1830	*F. fulgens*		

As each new species is discovered, the natural instinct of any plant breeder is to improve upon them. So it was that the British Hybridisers started their work. It is interesting to note the names and dates of the first introductions of some of these pioneers, to whom we should be grateful for producing the forerunners of the fantastic plants available today.

1832	Bunney	British	1862	Greene	British
1833	Roberts	British	1863	Weinrich	German
1836	Salter	British/French	1864	Fry	British
				L'Huillier	French
1838	Lowe	British	1865	Demay	French
1840	Epps	British	1866	Smith	British
	Harrison	British		Twrdy	German
	Youell	British	1867	Bland	British
	Mayle	British	1869	Carter	British
	Normald	British		Dixon	British
1841	May	British	1870	Williams	British
	Smith	British	1873	Stride	British
	Standish	British	1883	Rundle	British
1842	Knight	British	1887	Sankey	British
	Pince	British	1892	Veitch	British
	Potney	British	1904	Bonstedt	German
	Story	British	1911	Howlett	British
1843	Halley	British	1920	Spackman	American
	Turville	British	1929	Grenn	American
1844	Banks	British	1930	Hazard & Hazard	American
	Miller	British	1933	Evans & Reeves	American
1845	Miellez	French			
	Rogers	British	1934	York	British
1846	Barkway	British	1935	Berkeley Hort	American
	Bull	British		Wood	British
	Jennings	British	1937	Blackwell	British
1847	Wheeler	British	1938	Garson	American
1848	Lemoine	French		Niederhulzer	American
	Turner	British	1939	Reiter	American
1853	Coene	Belgian	1940	Nelson	American
	Crousse	French			
	Henderson	British			
1860	Cornelisen	Belgian			
	Rozaine-Boucharlat	French			

For the next two decades the production of new cultivars was almost totally in the hands of the American Hybridisers. It is to them that we owe our thanks for producing so many large-flowered, trailing fuchsias. Between the years 1941–1950 we are indebted to Brand; Faircio; Haag, W. & R.; Hanson; Hodges; Nutzinger; Nessier; Schnabel; Schmidt; Reedstrom; Tiret; Walker & Jones and Waltz. The following decade shows a similar American dominance with Brown-Soules; Chiles; Erickson; Jones; Kennett; Martin; Machado; Munkner; Peterson; Plummer; and Walker.

During these two decades the major British Hybridisers were Whiteman (1941), Travis (1951), and Thorne (1953).

The 1960s saw the resurgence of the British Hybridisers:

1961	Kucchier	American	1968	Steevens	Dutch
	Thornley	British	1969	Pugh	British
1962	Gagnoin	American	1970	Gorman	American
	Miller	British		Holmes	British
1963	Colville	British		Ryle	British
1964	Need	British		Senior	British
1965	Gadsby	British		Stubbs	American
	Paskesen	American	1971	Tolley	British
	Field	American		Handley	British
1966	Holmes	British.	1972	Clyne	British
	Prentice	American	1974	Tabraham	British
	Roe	British	1976	Palko	American
1967	De Groot	Dutch			
	Pennisi	American			
	Wilson	British			

No attempt has been made in the above list to include every Hybridiser, rather it consists of those who have presented us with either five or more cultivars or have been responsible for producing something really special.

And so on into the 1980s and 1990s. New names will appear when the history of the fuchsia for this period is recorded – names such as Beilby, Brazier, Bridgland, Burns, Clark, Dyos, Goulding, Hall, Heavens, Hobbs, Hobson, Mitchinson, Oxtoby, Redfern and Wright. There are many others, in many parts of the world, who are producing great plants – to leave any out is rather unfair.

Great strides are being made: new breaks with colour and form are being discovered; science is being used to unravel the complexities of genetics. Who knows what the ultimate result will be? In a way it will be a shame if our scientists reach the stage when they can forecast the result of the crossing of two cultivars or species – it is the uncertainty of what will be produced which gives the art of hybridisation its appeal.

In the latter part of the 1980s there was much anxiety regarding the large number of 'new' cultivars that were being produced – just how many of these cultivars are an improvement upon those that have gone before is the cause of much controversy. New breakthroughs are being made but whether these will stand the test of time remains to be seen.

When a history of the fuchsia is being written in the year 2050, how many of today's introductions will still be available? Glancing through the list of cultivars mentioned in this book, it is interesting to note that many of them are around a hundred years old:

Achievement	(Melville 1876)	Herald	(Sankey 1887)
Amy Lye	(Lye 1885)	Joy Patmore	(Turner 1861)
Autumnale	(Meteor 1880)	Lena	(Bunney 1862)
Beacon	(Bull 1871)	Lye's Unique	(Lye 1886)
Bon Accord	(Crousse 1861)	Marinka	(Rozaine-
Brilliant	(Bull 1865)		Boucharlat 1902)
Brutus	(Lemoine 1897)	Mrs W. Rundle	(Rundle 1883)
Clipper	(Lye 1887)	Rose of Castille	(Banks 1869)
Cloth of Gold	(Stafford 1863)	Thalia	(Turner 1855)
Countess of		Tom Thumb	(Baudinat 1850)
Aberdeen	(Forbes 1888)	Tom West	(Meillez 1853)
Display	(Smith 1881)		

No list of older cultivars would be complete without a mention of the *triphylla* type. As stated earlier, the fuchsia which was first brought to notice by Father Charles Plumier was named *Fuchsia triphylla coccinea*. The attractiveness of this fuchsia with its long tube has encouraged many hybridists over the years to produce cultivars with this form – the only problem being that *F. triphylla* is frost shy and so unfortunately are most of its progeny.

The leading hybridist with this type of fuchsia was undoubtedly Carl Bonstedt, a German who produced Traudchen Bonstedt, Mary, Koralle, Gottingen and Gartenmeister Bonstedt between 1904 and 1906. Today, many of our hybridists, realising the attractiveness of these terminal flowering forms, are concentrating upon them to produce interesting new cultivars.

As with all things, but perhaps more so in the world of horticulture, memories can be very fickle, labels bearing the names of plants can become detached and, rather than throw away an attractive plant, a new name is attached to it. And so the scientific value of a plant becomes debased. Attempts have been made over the years to record the names and descriptions of plants, and indeed the American Fuchsia Society is the International Registrar for the recording of fuchsia names. Those who have spent long hours sifting through old catalogues for descriptions deserve to be remembered, as indeed do those whose work has been published.

In 1844 Felix M. Porcher published *Le Fuchsia, son Histoire et sa Culture*. Within this first edition he was able to list some 300 species and varieties. Just four years later, in 1848, his second edition listed some 520 species and varieties. In 1883 the first book on fuchsias in English, *A Practical Treatise on Fuchsias* by Frederick Buss, was published. In 1936, *A Check List of Fuchsias* by E.O. Essig was published by the American Fuchsia Society. And in 1943 *A Revision of the Genus Fuchsia* by Philip A. Munz was produced. 1975 saw the publication of *A Check List of Species, Hybrids and Cultivars of the Genus Fuchsia* by Leo. B. Boullemier. Every effort is being made to maintain this book and to keep it up to date with recent introductions. 1982 saw the production of *Fuchsia Lexicon* by Ron Ewart – another publication essential for the enthusiast and which will be kept up to date.

There is no doubt that the success of the fuchsia, and its growth in popularity, has to a large extent been brought about by the formation of societies and groups. When people with similar interests get together to discuss their mutual 'hobby', the popularity of their subject spreads – this is certainly so with the fuchsia. In 1929 the American Fuchsia Society was formed in California. As a result of the enthusiasm of the early pioneers, and their visits to Europe to collect plants of the species and cultivars which were then available, the desire to grow fuchsias spread and new cultivars were produced. The British had been the real pioneers in producing new cultivars but it was not until 1938 that a small group of enthusiasts decided to form the Fuchsia Society, later to be known as the British Fuchsia Society. These founder members – Mr W. Whiteman, Lady Boothby and Revd Dr H.A. Brown – sowed the seed which has grown into a very thriving society with around six thousand members. If one adds to that the members of societies affiliated to the British Fuchsia Society who are not themselves members of the BFS, then the number of those interested in the growing of fuchsias runs into tens of thousands.

The history of the fuchsia may be shrouded in doubts and uncertainties but there can certainly be no doubt as to what the future will hold. It is impossible to see anything other than a gathering of interest and a continuation of the desire to grow and admire a flower which had such a humble beginning.

2

Classification

SPECIES

No book on fuchsias would be complete without reference to the plants from which all of the modern cultivars have emanated. It would probably be fair to say that a good knowledge of the fuchsia species is confined to very few people around the world. It is a subject which has fascinated many over the years and yet to even more the subject seems to retain a mystique which makes it almost taboo. However, as knowledge of the existence of fuchsias goes back a mere two hundred years, it should be possible to obtain complete authenticated records of all those members of the genus *fuchsia* known to man. Much work was done on the subject by Professor Philip A. Munz, who published his work, *The Revision of the Genus Fuchsia* in 1943. In this study, 100 different species were recognised as making up the genus *fuchsia* and these were subdivided into seven sections.

Since the original publication of this work further studies have been carried out by Dr Paul E. Berry, Dr Peter H. Raven and Dennis Breedlove, as a result of which the number of sections has been increased to nine and many of the original errors in naming have been corrected. It is to be hoped that their work will result in the correct naming of many of the species now available in Britain.

Section 1   *Quelusia* (Argentina, Brazil and Chile)

F. bracelinae	F. magellanica var. alba
F. campus-portoi	F. magellanica var. macrostema
F. coccinea	F. regia
F. magellanica	F. regia var. alpestris
F. regia var. regia	

Section 2   *Fuchsia* (Andes and Central America)

F. abrupta	F. ampliata
F. andrei	F. austromontana
F. ayavacensis	F. boliviana
F. canescens	F. caucana

15

The Distribution of the species Fuchsia

Section 1 *Quelusia*
Section 2 *Fuchsia*
Section 3 *Kierschlegeria*
Section 4 *Skinnera*
Section 5 *Helmsleyella*

Section 6 *Schuffia*
Section 7 *Encliandra*
Section 8 *Jimenezia*
Section 9 *Ellobium*

F. ceracea
F. concertifolia
F. corollata
F. crassistipula
F. decussata
F. dependens
F. fontinalis
F. gehrigeri
F. harlingii
F. hirtella
F. llewelynii
F. macropetala
F. macrostigma
F. mathewsii
F. orientalis
F. pallescens
F. pilosa

F. cochabambana
F. coriacifolia
F. corymbiflora
F. cautrecasii
F. denticulata
F. ferreyrae
F. furfuracea
F. glaberrima
F. hartwegii
F. lechmanii
F. loxensis
F. macrophylla
F. magdalenae
F. nigricans
F. ovalis
F. petiolaris
F. polyantha

F. *pringsheimii*
F. *rivularis*
F. *sanmartina*
F. *scherffiana*
F. *simplicicaulis*
F. *sylvatica*
F. *triphylla*
F. *venusta*
F. *vulcanica*

F. *putamayensis*
F. *sanctae-rosea*
F. *scabriuscula*
F. *sessilifolia*
F. *steyermarkii*
F. *tincta*
F. *vargasiana*
F. *verrucosa*
F. *wurdackii*

Section   *Kierschlegeria* (Chile)

F. *lycioides*

Section 4   *Skinnera* (New Zealand and Tahiti)

F. *colensoi*
F. *excorticata*
F. *procumbens*

F. *cyrtandroides*
F. *perscandens*

Section 5   *Hemsleyella* (Bolivia and Venezuela)

F. *apetala*
F. *chloroloba*
F. *huanucoensis*
F. *insignis*
F. *membranacea*
F. *pitaloensis*
F. *tillettiana*

F. *cestroides*
F. *garleppiana*
F. *inflata*
F. *juntasensis*
F. *nana*
F. *salcifolia*
F. *tunariensis*

Section 6   *Schuffia* (Central America and Mexico)

F. *arborescens*

F. *paniculata*

Section 7   *Encliandra* (Central America and Mexico)

F. *x bacillaris*
F. *encliandra ssp tetradactyla*
F. *microphylla ssp microphylla*
F. *parviflora*
F. *thymifolia ssp thymifolia*

F. *encliandra ssp encliandra*
F. *microphylla ssp hemsleyana*
F. *microphylla ssp minutiflora*
F. *thymifolia ssp minimiflora*

Section 8   *Jimenezia* (Costa Rica and Panama)

F. *jimenezia*

Section 9   *Ellobium* (Central America and Mexico)

F. *fulgens*
F. *splendens*

F. *decidua*

Habitat

The most important information to be gleaned from such early studies concerns the natural habitat of the species, the climatic conditions that the plants prefer, which must be recreated if they are to flourish elsewhere. Even so, the interbreeding of these species in conditions contrary to their natural habitat has produced our modern cultivars which have adapted more and more to the previously alien climate of Britain.

The majority of the species, apart from a small group found in New Zealand, are found growing in Central and Southern America, much of this area being within the tropical zones. Yet the plants are not tender tropical shrubs which can only be cultivated in the warmest and dampest greenhouses, as the growing areas within these tropical zones are usually at sufficient altitude to reduce the overall temperature. The high, moisture-laden mountain slopes with, at times, dense foliage, should give some idea of the conditions in which the plants thrive. Moist air around the plant will give a good healthy look to the foliage; dappled or shaded sunshine will enhance the colour of the blooms; a temperature in excess of freezing but without direct dry heat will encourage luscious growth.

There are some varieties, however, which are considered to be hardy, and can be left out in gardens to take their chance against the freezing temperatures of winter. Such plants were originally discovered around the Magellan Straits, growing at high altitude in areas of Southern Chile. As the climate in the milder parts of Britain and Ireland is similar to their natural habitat, they have easily become established within those areas. The marvellous sight of glowing red hedges has prompted many to the growing of fuchsias as a hobby.

Even within one area there can be considerable variation in the shape and size of plants of the same genus. Taking as an example the plants of fuchsias native to New Zealand, there is a wide diversity of form. The four native species vary from *F. excorticata,* which grows into a spreading tree that can attain a height of over 35 feet (11m), to the woody creeper *F. procumbens,* which has very long slender stems and flowers freely in very sandy ground. The small erect flower of *F. procumbens* is devoid of petals, but with its greenish-yellow tube and bright blue pollen on the stamens, it is particularly attractive.

Species

It is possible, when travelling around the country, to visit the greenhouses of fuchsia enthusiasts who have become absolutely hooked on the species. A collection of the various types, growing together in ideal conditions, with their roots free to roam in the border, is certainly a sight well worth seeing. Many growers, although fascinated by the shapes and sizes of flowers available, are rather put off from growing these plants because of the extra space that they appear to need. Some very good specimens are presented on the show benches, growing in fairly large pots. Such plants always cause a considerable amount of interest and a well-grown specimen is likely to be a strong contender for the premier award.

Unfortunately the number of different species seen on the show bench is rather limited. There are two possible reasons for this: a desire only to show those which give a good account of themselves and produce eye-catching foliage and flowers; or the lack of choice that there appears to be even at specialised fuchsia nurseries around the country. It is a fact of life that even when such plants are obtainable at nurseries many are incorrectly named – a system which is perpetuated as few people are sufficiently qualified to change it.

What follows is a brief look at some of the species seen on the show bench, which are considered to be sufficiently easy to grow and very rewarding in the quantity and quality of the flowers they produce.

F. procumbens

I have no hesitation in putting this one in first place, as it seems to fascinate everyone who sees it. It is found growing naturally on the shore line of New Zealand, and therefore requires a compost with a very open and sandy texture. It is best described as a trailing or creeping fuchsia which sends down roots from long thin stems as it spreads across the ground. The root system is not very strong but this habit of rooting along the branches helps to build up a good strong plant. It is very useful trailing over the edge of a pot or for use in hanging pots or baskets.

The flowers are quite small and face upwards from the trailing branches. The tube is a yellowy-green and the sepals a dark ruby red. There are no petals, but the blue pollen which can be seen on the ends of the stamens is an attractive feature.

The quantity of seed that is set also adds to the plant's appeal.

The seed pods should always be left on any of the species but with *procumbens* the seed pods are much larger than the flowers from which they were formed. They grow almost to the size of a small damson plum and when ripe have the same sort of colouring. The pods should be left on the plant until absolutely ripe, when they can be collected and then kept until the following spring in a dry place. In the spring, split the pods and sow the seed on the surface of your usual compost. Keep the seeds moist and warm, and within a short period of time you will have a good collection of *procumbens* seedlings – which are true to form. If seed is simply spread on the surface of compost in a hanging basket there will be little need to do much more to obtain an excellent basket for later in the season.

F. fulgens

Another of the species that you will see on the show benches, this is one that causes the spectators to gasp in astonishment. As there are a number of natural variants of this species, it is sometimes difficult to gain acceptance for them in the species classes at some shows.

The main feature of these plants is the luxurious foliage. The large green leaves, in a well grown plant, will completely cover the whole of the plant – the loss of a few leaves lower down will give it a very bare look. At the ends of branches bunches of very long tubed flowers are formed, and again it is necessary to leave on the plant any seed pods which form when the flowers have died.

One of the rules regarding the showing of species is that they should be grown with a minimum of formal training. With the *fulgens* it is necessary, in order to obtain a good bushy plant, to stop the growths on two or three occasions. This will give sufficient branches to produce an excellent shrubby plant. As with most species it is important to allow a fairly long period of time, perhaps up to twelve weeks, between the final 'stopping' of the plant and show day. Actually, as seed pods are permissible, in fact desirable, on a plant, the timing of species for show purposes is not so critical as long as you have allowed sufficient time for the flowers to come out completely and the first seed pods form.

The root system of the *fulgens* is rather extensive and a fairly large pot, say 8 or 9 inches (20 to 23cm), will be required for a two or three year old plant. The tuberous root is very similar to a dahlia and may be overwintered out of the pots provided that it is kept frost free. For the best colour in leaves and flowers it is advisable to grow these plants in conditions similar to their natural habitat – dappled shade.

In fairness the names of some of the natural variants of *F. fulgens* need to be mentioned. Many of these are seen on the show benches and are the cause of much agonising on the part of the judges and the show officials. They have the same characteristics as *F. fulgens*, with the same large, luxurious leaves and brilliant flowers of many different hues. *F. fulgens carminata*, *F. fulgens gesneriana* (perhaps the most frequently seen), *F. fulgens rubra grandiflora* (as grand as its name suggests), and *F. fulgens multiflora pumilla*.

F. splendens (syn. F. cordifolia)

This plant can grow to about three feet (1m) in height and has very attractive flowers, which are produced singly from the leaf axils. The tube of the flower is a fairly bright red (carrot red) but the sepals and petals are an attractive green colour. The tube has a very distinctive flattening along about two thirds of its length.

This species does not appreciate restriction of its root system and when potting on it is advisable to go into larger pots fairly quickly. If you are impatient to see flowers on your fuchsias then this is an excellent plant to grow. It comes into flower early and remains in flower for a long period. Although it appreciates a shady part of the garden it will take full sun – try growing it in the open garden (in its pot), as it seems to appreciate this sort of situation.

F. arborescens

The question asked when this one appears on the show bench is 'Is that a fuchsia?' In its natural habitat it grows as a shrub or small tree sometimes attaining a height of 20 feet (6 to 7m) or more. With its highly distinctive flowers, it is sometimes referred to as the 'lilac fuchsia'. The official description states that it flowers on terminal cymose panicles. The individual flowers are very small but this is compensated for by the quantity on each panicle. The leaves are very long and reasonably thin, but it has an unfortunate tendency to lose its lower leaves which gives it a rather bare look at the base.

To obtain a bushy plant, two or three stops are necessary although I have found that it tends, occasionally, to object to this and 'sulks' for a while before recommencing its growth. After flowering, the seed pods which remain on the plant resemble a bunch of elderberries although harder and shinier. As with all species for show purposes the minimum of training is required – nevertheless it is possible, as was witnessed at one national show, to grow this plant as a standard. Different – and a useful talking point.

F. sanctae-rosea

This is another very attractive species occasionally seen on the show bench. It produces its leaves in fours and as it is very close jointed there will always be ample foliage – the lack of foliage on some of the other types is a common complaint. It always produces a plentiful supply of flowers which are produced at each leaf axil. The unopened flowers are tipped with green; once opened, the flowers have green-tipped vermilion sepals, and vermilion tubes. The seed pods are mistletoe green flushed vermilion. If grown in the greenhouse the species will take both full sun and partial shade.

F. simplicicaulis

The natural habitat of this species is Peru, where it is found growing some 7000 feet above sea-level. In this habitat it builds up into a large shrub growing to a height of some fourteen feet (4½m), using other plants for support. It is fairly free branching so some formal training (not too much or you will lose favour with the judges) will be needed to produce the type of shape required. Careful staking early in the season is necessary to produce that good shape.

The flowers appear on terminal racemes, usually accompanied by some reduced leaves. The unopened flowers are neyron rose in colour and the very long tube is neyron rose maturing to a crimson. The petals are crimson. Plants with this type of flowering, i.e. terminal racemes, need longer from the final stopping of the plant until they flower, so allow a good fourteen weeks to be safe.

F. regia

This is best described as a climbing shrub reaching a height of some fourteen feet (4½m) using other plants for support – it will take over a greenhouse if properly cared for. Although it grows and flowers well, the flowers are somewhat smaller than some of the more luxurious-looking fuchsias. It prefers not to branch out on its own so will need a certain amount of assistance. Stopping the growing tips will give a bushier plant but it will require training to a trellis-type structure to keep it within bounds. It has a very strong root system so it will require permanently planting in the greenhouse border. This can hardly be described as a show plant, but it is nevertheless very attractive.

F. magellanica

The original plants of this species were found on the mountain slopes of the southernmost part of South America, so it is little wonder that they found the climate in Ireland and southern Britain so much to their liking. With its small red and purple flower, this is the plant that many people think of as being the 'real' fuchsia. It is easily grown and is very useful when making hedges. It is very hardy and will come up year after year producing a multitude of flowers from very early in the season. Please do not think that they are all red and purple.

Although the red and purple flower is the most popular, it is not the only type available. *Magellanica alba* (alba meaning white) has a small pinkish-white flower, and many plants which have the name *magellanica* have variegated foliage. In all there are some forty differing forms of this species, each with variation in flowers, shape or foliage. They are useful plants to have and are easily increased from cuttings.

Encliandra Group

Within this section of the fuchsia species there is a fairly large number of plants which have miniature flowers and very small leaves. The growth on these plants is normally very slender although it is possible to grow some very large, attractive bushy plants which will flower abundantly. They are very easily propagated, as any small tips removed will form roots in a very short space of time. After flowering, small shiny black seed pods are produced which help to enhance the beauty of the plant late in the season. In most shows nowadays there are classes especially for plants of the *Encliandra* group.

For showing, these should be grown with a minimum of formal training, but some very exciting shapes can be built up. Plants grown as pillars, or trained in circles around wire, or as miniature standards can be very effective indeed. Although they may not be acceptable on the show bench they can, nevertheless, give a considerable amount of personal satisfaction and enjoyment, which is in many cases the object of the exercise.

This is only a selection of the available species. I would suggest that anyone who is really interested in this side of fuchsia growing should contact one of the real species enthusiasts – visit their gardens, ask questions, seek out species from the specialist fuchsia growers and keep asking for more and more of them until it becomes obvious to the nurseryman that there is need to stock a wider selection of the plants from which all our modern cultivars have originated.

RECOMMENDED CULTIVARS

The following is a list of cultivars recommended for their appearance and ease of cultivation. The asterisk marks those plants considered hardy enough to withstand an average winter outdoors.

Abbé Farges★   (Lemoine 1901) Semi-double. Sepals light cerise; corolla rosy lilac. The flowers are small, but are profusely produced. Height approximately 2 feet (60 cm).
Achievement★   (Melville 1876) Single. Tube and sepals red; corolla violet to red. Spreading and self branching growth. Leaves have a slight yellow cast. Height 2 feet 6 inches (75 cm).
Alice Hoffman★   (Klese 1911) Semi-double. Tube and sepals rose pink; corolla white veined with rose. Makes a very compact and bushy plant. Height 18 inches (45 cm).
Alison Ewart   (Roe 1976) Single. Tube and sepals neyron rose; corolla mauve with a faint pink flush. Small flowers freely produced. Upright, self branching cultivar excellent for small pot culture.
Alwin   (Clyne 1976) Semi-double. Tube and sepals neyron

rose; corolla white veined red. Very floriferous, with medium flowers.

Amy Lye (Lye 1885) Single. Tube creamy white; sepals white with green tips; corolla coral orange cerise. Upright, bushy and vigorous growth which responds to training.

Annabel (Ryle 1978) Double. Tube and sepals white flushed neyron rose; corolla rich creamy white. Large flowers freely produced. Soft green foliage.

Ann H. Tripp (Clark 1982) Single. Sepals white; corolla white, very lightly veined pink. Seedling from Lady Isobel Barnett.

F. arborescens (Mexico) Tube rose red to magenta; sepals reddish to wine purple; corolla lilac lavender. Flowers in corymbose panicles held erect.

Auntie Jinks (Wilson 1970) Single. Tube pink-red; sepals white edged cerise; corolla purple with white shading. Smallish blooms but extremely floriferous and attractive.

Autumnale (Meteor 1880) Single. Tube and sepals scarlet rose; corolla purple. Medium flowers but late coming into bloom. Grown mainly for its very attractive foliage – gold and coppery red, yellow, dark red and salmon. With a rather stiff habit to its growth, it tends to appear rather more horizontal than vertical.

Barbara (Tolley 1973) Single. Tube and sepals pale pink; corolla tangerine pink. Prolific flowers of medium size. Will take full sun.

Barry's Queen (Sheppard 1980) Single. Tube and sepals rhodamine pink; corolla amethyst violet. Sport of Border Queen and identical in flower, but foliage is a brilliant yellow. Very showy.

Beacon★ (Bull 1871) Single. Tube and sepals deep pink; corolla bright mauvish pink. Waxy dark green foliage. Makes an excellent bush or standard. Self branching. Height 3 feet (90 cm).

Bealings (Goulding 1983) Double. Sepals waxy white, ageing to faintest pink; corolla intense violet. Free-flowering.

Billy Green (1966) A *triphylla*-type fuchsia. Single. Corolla and sepals pinkish salmon. Upright growth.

Blush of Dawn (Martin 1962) Double. Tube and sepals cream with dawn pink on the reverse of each sepal; corolla pale lavender then silver-blue. A trailer so will, with patience, make a good basket. Delightful pastel colouring.

Bobby Shaftoe (Ryle 1970) Semi-double. Tube and sepals a clear frosty white; flushed with palest pink. Mid to light green foliage. Prolific flowerer and an excellent show variety.

Bobby Wingrove   (Wingrove 1966) Single. Sepals pinkish red, tipped green; corolla turkey red. Self branching compact bush. Blooms continuously.

F. boliviana   (Bolivia) Sepals dark red and reflexing; corolla varying from light to dark red. Upright shrubby growth.

Bon Accorde   (Crousse 1861) Single. Tube and sepals waxy white; corolla pale purple on white. Flowers small, and held upright.

Border Queen   (Ryle 1974) Single. Sepals rhodamine pink, tipped with green; corolla amethyst violet flushed pale pink with dark pink veins, fading to white at base. Excellent free-blooming plant.

Bouffant   (Tiret 1949) Single. Tube and sepals red; corolla white, veined rosy red. Large blooms which are freely produced. Cascading growth.

Brilliant   (Bull 1865) Single. Tube and sepals red with recurving; corolla violet, maturing to magenta. Long flowers, fairly large. A vigorous grower.

Brookwood Joy   (Gilbert 1983) Sepals white outside, tipped green, with blush pink underside; corolla hyacinth blue, marbled phlox pink. Deep pink stamens. Large fully double flowers.

Brutus*   (Lemoine 1897) Single. Sepals rich cerise; corolla dark purple, almost black. Strong bushy growth. Height 3 feet (90 cm).

Cambridge Louie   (Napthen 1977) Single. Sepals pinky orange; corolla rosy pink with darker edges. Small light green foliage.

Cascade   (Lagen 1937) Single. Tube and sepals white flushed carmine; corolla rose bengal. Light to medium green foliage. Cascading growth, self branching. Makes an excellent basket but tends to flower at the ends of the branches.

Catherine Bartlett   (Roe 1983) Single. Short white tube flushed pale rose; corolla beautiful shade of rose, lighter at base. Very dainty, very floriferous Light green foliage.

Celia Smedley   (Roe 1972) Single. Sepals neyron rose; corolla currant red. Large flowers and strong growth.

Chang   (Hazard 1946) Single. Tube and sepals orange with a hint of cerise; corolla bright orange. Small but plentiful flowers. Extremely attractive colour combination.

Charlie Gardiner   (Goulding 1982) Single. Tube carmine. Reflexing sepals reddish cerise; corolla rose apricot. Very free-flowering and will make an excellent basket.

Checkerboard (Walker Jones 1948) Single. Tube red; sepals start red and then abruptly change to white; corolla deeper red. Very free-flowering

Christmas Elf (Gentry 1972) Single. Tube bright red; reflexing sepals bright red; corolla almost pure white with red veins. Small dark green foliage. Self branching, dwarf growth. Excellent for exhibiting in small pots.

Cliffs Unique (Gadsby 1976) Double. Short thick light pink tube; sepals waxy white flushed with pink; corolla gentian blue maturing to light violet pink. Medium-sized blooms which are carried semi-erect.

Clipper (Lye 1897) Single. Tube and recurving sepals scarlet cerise; corolla rich claret red. Medium green foliage. Upright, vigorous bushy plant.

Cloth of Gold (Stafford 1863) Single. Tube and sepals red; corolla purple. Golden yellow foliage which ages to green with a bronze-like flush, underside reddish. Grown for its foliage as flowers are late in the season.

Cloverdale Jewel (Gadsby 1974) Semi-double. Tube and sepals neyron rose; corolla wisteria blue with rose pink veins. Upright strong growth. Very floriferous. Carries its blooms over a long period.

Cloverdale Pearl (Gadsby 1974) Single. Sepals rhodamine pink; corolla white with pink veins. An upright self branching bush, which is often seen on the show bench. Very floriferous and easy to train.

Coachman (Bright 1910–20) Single. Tube and sepals pale salmon; corolla orange-vermilion. Flowers in clusters. The pale green soft foliage is very attractive. Vigorous grower so useful for large structures.

Constance (Berkeley Horticultural Nurseries 1935) Double. Tube and sepals pale pink; corolla rosy mauve with pink tints at base of petals. Free-flowering upright growing plant.

F. cordifolia (*syn. F. splendens*) (Guatemala) Tube dark scarlet; sepals scarlet with green tips; corolla combination of green, yellow and white.

F. corymbiflora (Peru) Long scarlet tube; scarlet sepals; corolla coral red. Long flowers borne in large terminal racemes. Needs plenty of root space.

Countess of Aberdeen (Forbes 1888) Single. Tube and sepals soft pink; corolla creamy white with pink flush. Flowers small but very freely produced.

Crackerjack (Fuchsia-la 1961) Single to semi-double. Tube and sepals white with hint of pink; corolla pale blue then mauve. Very strong grower. Excellent in a basket as it is a natural trailer.

Curly Q (Kennett 1961) Single. Tube and sepals cream; corolla violet purple. Charming small flowers. Its name comes from the fact that the sepals roll into little circles which lie back against the tube.

Daisy Bell (Raiser unknown–introduced in 1977) Single. Tube white shading to green at base; corolla vermillion shading to orange at the base of the petals. Foliage light to medium green. Natural trailer which will make excellent full or half baskets.

Dark Eyes (Erickson 1958) Double. Tube and sepals deep red. Corolla rich violet blue. Flowers medium free.

F. denticulata (Peru and Bolivia) Long reddish pink tube; sepals reddish pink tipped with green; corolla red. Very large foliage. Rather late flowering and requires additional heat. Strong upright bush.

Derby Imp (Gadsby 1974) Single. Tube and sepals crimson; corolla violet blue. An early flowering variety with dwarf free-branching growth. Excellent for use in classes calling for small pots.

Display★ (Smith 1881) Single. Sepals rose pink; corolla deep cerise pink. Medium full green foliage. Very free-flowering. Good strong upright growth. Self branching. Excellent for use when growing large structures. Height 2 feet 6 inches (75 cm).

Dollar Princess (Lemoine 1912) Double. Tube and sepals cerise; corolla purple. Medium green foliage. Good strong upright growth. Self branching. Early flowering.

Dusky Beauty (Ryle 1981) Single. Sepals neyron rose; corolla pale purple with pink cast and deeper pink edges. Small flowers but very prolific.

Dusky Rose (Waltz 1960) Double. Tube and sepals pink, almost coral; corolla rose, deeper when mature. Very full flowers with ruffled edges which give it a very attractive appearance. A natural trailer which will make a good basket.

Eden Lady (Ryle 1975) Single. Sepals amaranth rose, deeper underneath with the whole shading to white at tips; corolla hyacinth blue. Sister seedling to Border Queen.

Eleanor Leytham (Roe 1974) Single. Tube and sepals pinkish white; corolla pink with deeper pink on the edges of the petals. Small foliage medium green. Very small blooms but very free flowering. Excellent for use in 'small pot culture' classes.

Estelle Marie   (Newton 1973) Single. Sepals greenish white with green tips; corolla blue violet. Exhibition variety.

Falling Stars   (Reiter 1941) Single. Tube and sepals red; corolla dusky red (almost brown). Medium-sized flowers freely produced. Cascading type growth.

Fascination   (Lemoine 1905 – originally known as Emile de Wildeman) Double. Tube and sepals bright red; corolla rose pink. Vigorous grower which can be useful for all types of large structure work.

Fiery Spider   (Munkner 1960) Single. Tube pale carmine – long and thin; sepals pale salmon pink with green tips; corolla crimson, flushed with orange. A natural trailer which is vigorous and free-flowering.

Flirtation Waltz   (Waltz 1962) Double. Tube and sepals white; corolla delicate shell pink. An excellent bush which needs only a minimum of training.

Flying Cloud   (Reiter 1949) Double. Tube and sepals white with green tips; corolla white with faint pink splashes at the base of the petals. Vigorous, upright, bushy growth.

Frank Unsworth   (Clark 1982) Double. Short white tube; white sepals which fly back covering the tube; corolla white with slight pink flush at base of petals. Small dark green foliage. Lax growth so makes an excellent basket.

F. fulgens   (Mexico 1828) Long tube light vermilion red; sepals yellowy green with red base; corolla bright vermilion. Large light sage green foliage. Tuberous roots. An upright shrub which, with good root room, makes a magnificent specimen.

F. fulgens var. gesneriana   Similar in description to *F. fulgens*, but the flower tube is shorter and the growth is rather more lax.

F. fulgens var. rubra grandiflora   Perhaps the most beautiful of the varieties of *fulgens*, with very long tubed flowers. Similar habit of growth.

Garden News★   (Handley 1978) Double. Sepals frosty rose pink; corolla magenta rose blending to rose at base. A relatively new cultivar which has created a great impression. Height 2 feet 6 inches (75 cm).

Gartenmeister Bonstedt   (Bonstedt 1905) Single. Orange tubular flowers with blue-green foliage. This is a *triphylla*-type plant which will need protection under cover during the winter.

General Monk   (French, date unknown) Double. Tube and sepals cerise rose; corolla blue ageing to mauvish blue. Prolific bloomer which will make a very neat bush with a minimum of training.

Genii (Jeanne)★ (Reiter 1951) Single. Tube and sepals cerise; corolla rich violet. Foliage pale to medium yellowish green when growing outdoors in full sun. Height 3 feet (90cm)

Golden Marinka (Weber 1955) Single. A sport from Marinka with identical flowers – red sepals with darker red corolla. Its pendulous growth makes it perfect for baskets.

Green 'n Gold (Rasmussen 1954) Single. Delightful coral pink self. Flowers are profuse, bell-shaped and borne in clusters. Small foliage with cream and yellow colouring provided it is grown in full sun. Sport from Glendale. Bushy growth.

Harry Gray (Dunnett 1981) Double. Tube and sepals rose pink; corolla white shading to rose pink. Compact small to medium-sized blooms. Very floriferous. A self branching trailer so ideal for use in hanging containers.

Heidi Ann (Smith 1969) Double. Tube and sepals crimson cerise; corolla bright lilac. Medium-sized flowers. Very free-flowering.

Herald★ (Sankey 1887) Single. Sepals scarlet; corolla deep purple. Foliage light green, very attractive. Vigorous grower which can be trained to many shapes. Height 3 feet (90cm).

Hidcote Beauty (Webb 1949) Tube creamy white; sepals creamy waxy white with green tips; corolla pale salmon pink. Medium-sized leaves pale to medium green. Upright bushy and vigorous in growth, and can be encouraged into making a good basket. Very free-flowering

Hula Girl (Paskessen 1972) Double. Tube and sepals deep rose pink; corolla white shading to pink at base of petals. Foliage is medium green with red veins and red on the underside. Very free-flowering – a natural trailer so recommended for baskets.

Icecap (Gadsby 1968) Single to semi-double. Tube and sepals bright red; corolla white with cerise veining. Small to medium-sized blooms upward looking. Excellent for all bush type classes in shows.

Jack Acland (Haag 1952) Single. Tube and sepals bright pink; corolla deep rose maturing to pink. Floriferous. Good strong upright bush.

Jack Shahan (Tiret 1948) Single. Tube and sepals pale rose bengal; corolla rose bengal. Large flowers profusely produced over a long period. Rather lax growth but can be trained as an upright bush. Makes a fine basket which will give pleasure over a long period.

Joans Delight (Gadsby 1977) Single. Tube and sepals crimson; corolla violet blue. Small flower. Dwarf growth, self branching. Excellent for use in small pots.

Joan Smith (Thorne 1958) Single. Tube and sepals flesh pink; corolla soft pink. Extremely vigorous upright growth. Excellent for large structures.

Joy Patmore (Turner 1861) Single. Sepals pure white; Corolla rich carmine. Excellent show variety. Can be grown in a variety of shapes, being very easy to train. An eye-catching cultivar.

Kathy Louise (Antonelli 1963) Double. Tube and sepals carmine red; corolla rosy lilac with rose pink veins. Rather loose medium-sized blooms. Dark green foliage. Vigorous but will require a lot of pinching to make it into a basket. Its natural style of growth is trailing.

Ken Jennings (Roe 1982) Single. Sepals rhodamine pink; Corolla Tyrian purple. Strong bushy grower.

Koralle (Bonstedt 1905 – Sometimes called Coralle) *Triphylla*-type cultivar with tube, sepals and corolla salmon orange. Foliage is sage green with veins of a paler shade. Free-flowering vigorous grower.

La Campanella (Blackwell 1968) Semi-double. Tube white, faintly tinged pink; sepals white on top, slightly tinged pink on the underside; corolla imperial purple with some cerise veining. Small to medium-sized blooms are produced in profusion. Self cleaning. Lax growth but very vigorous once it gets going. An excellent cultivar for baskets.

Lady Isobel Barnett (Gadsby 1971) Single. Corolla rose purple; sepals rose red. Extremely floriferous variety.

Lady Thumb★ (Roe 1967) Single. Sepals reddish-carmine; corolla white, slightly veined carmine. Small flowers freely produced. A sport from Tom Thumb which has a similar dwarf growing habit. Height 12–18 inches (30–45 cm).

Lakeland Princess (Mitchinson 1981) Single. Short carmine tube; sepals white, flushed carmine at outside base, corolla spectrum violet, white at the base of each petal. Upright growth. Medium-sized flowers freely produced.

Lakeside (Thornley 1968) Single or semi-double. Tube and sepals deep pink; corolla light blue with pink veining, changing to lilac on maturity. Best described as a free-growing floriferous trailer. Excellent for all types of basket work.

Lena★ (Bunney 1862) Semi-double or double. Sepals pale

flesh pink; corolla rosy magenta. Although this is a hardy variety, it is often used in baskets. Good strong growth, so can be used in any situation. Height 18 inches (45 cm).

Lena Dalton (Reimers 1953) Sepals pale pink; corolla crispy blue. Medium-sized flowers. Dark green foliage. Will make a very nice neat shape.

Leverkusen (Hartnauer 1928) A *triphylla*-type cultivar which has clusters of long tubed cerise flowers. Unfortunately this plant reacts rapidly to any change of temperature or atmosphere by dropping its flowers and buds. Any exhibitor who gets this very attractive variety to the show bench in good form deserves special commendation. Nevertheless a lovely plant to grow.

Lindisfarne (Ryle-Atkinson 1974) Semi-double. Sepals pale pink; corolla rich dark violet. Flowers small but prolific.

Little Beauty (Raiser, date unknown) Single. Tube and sepals flesh pink; corolla lavender blue. Small flowers but very free and very early. Produces its best colour when grown in the shade.

Lyes Unique (Lye 1886) Single. Tube and sepals waxy white (rather fat tube); corolla salmon orange. An upright quick grower excellent for standard work. The colouring of the tube is a very distinctive feature of many of Lye's introductions.

Margaret★ (Wood 1937) Double. Tube and sepals rose; corolla mauve. A strong growing hardy variety with large flowers. Self branching and vigorous. Height 4 feet (1.2 m).

Margaret Brown★ (Wood 1949) Single. Tube and sepals rose pink; corolla rose bengal. Lightish green foliage. An excellent variety which 'drips' with flowers throughout a long season. Height 3 feet (90 cm).

Margaret Pilkington (Clark 1984) Single. Tube and sepals waxy white; corolla bishop's violet. Very free-flowering. Excellent show bench potential.

Margaret Roe (Gadsby 1968) Single. Tube and sepals rosy red; corolla pale violet purple. Very free-flowering. Sister seedling to Lady Isobel Barnett.

Marin Glow (Reedstrom 1954) Single. Tube and sepals pale waxy white; corolla imperial rich purple. Medium green foliage. An excellent plant for all purposes.

Marinka (Rozaine-Boucharlat 1902) Single. Tube and sepals red; corolla a slightly darker red. Very free-flowering, with medium-sized blooms. Trailing growth is excellent for baskets. Often considered to be the yardstick by which all other baskets are measured. Produced a sport – Golden Marinka.

Mary (Bonstedt 1905) A *triphylla*-type. Brilliant scarlet flowers with long tubes. The foliage is dark green and narrow. Makes an upright bush and is very distinctive. Not the easiest of plants to grow, but is always worth trying.

Mephisto (Reiter 1941) Single. Tube and sepals scarlet; corolla crimson red. The blooms are small and compact. Extremely vigorous growth upright and bushy. Free-flowering.

Micky Goult (Roe 1981) Single. Short white tube; short broad sepals white on top, very pale pink underneath. Flowers very early – small but floriferous.

F. microphylla (Mexico) Tube deep red; sepals red; corolla rosy pink. When grown under glass flowers can be almost white. Flowers very small.

Mieke Meursing (Hopwood 1968) Single to semi-double. Sepals red; corolla pale pink with deeper pink veining. A perfect variety to start with as it will form a perfect shape with very little effort. Prolific flowerer.

Mini Rose (de Graffe 1983) Single. Sepals pointed – very pale rose; corolla dark rose. Very small flowers but very profuse.

Mipam (Gubler 1976) Single. Tube pale carmine; sepals carmine pink; corolla magenta pink. Medium flower, very floriferous.

Miss California (Hodges 1950) Single or semi-double. Tube and sepals white becoming pale pink with deep pink stripes. Very long pointed sepals. Corolla white with wash of pink on maturing, pink veins. A very strong upright grower with thin stems which encourage it to take on a pendulous form. Good for baskets or as a weeping standard.

Mr A. Huggett (Raiser, date unknown) Single. Tube and sepals scarlet; corolla mauvish pink. Very floriferous and will make a good shaped plant with the minimum of attention.

Mrs Lovell Swisher (Evans-Reeves 1942) Single. Tube and sepals pink or ivory with a flush of pink; the underside of the sepals is pink; corolla carmine or rose red. Copious supply of dainty flowers on an upright bush.

Mrs Marshall (Jones 1862) Single. Tube and sepals creamy white; corolla rosy cerise. Medium sized blooms. Small to medium green serrated leaves. A vigorous, upright, self branching bushy plant. Free-flowering and easy to grow.

Mrs W. Rundle (Rundle 1883) Single. Tube and sepals a

waxy pale rose; corolla orange crimson. Flowers largish and long. Very free. Light green foliage. A lax growing plant which will make a magnificent weeping standard or hanging basket.

Muriel   (Raiser, date unknown) Single. Tube and sepals scarlet, sepals with green tips; corolla bluish magenta. Medium-sized bloom. Vigorous, rather lax growth so will make a good basket or weeping standard.

Nancy Lou   (Stubbs 1971) Double. Tube and sepals white or soft pink (depending upon the amount of sun); corolla brilliant white. Upright and compact growth.

Nellie Nuttall   (Roe 1977) Single. Very small brilliant red tube; small sepals deep crimson; corolla white with red veining. Very prolific bloomer and very early.

Northway   (Golics 1976) Single. Tube and sepals pale pink; corolla cherry red. Small compact blooms. Upright bushy growth, self branching and free-flowering. Makes a good bush but with parentage of La Campanella will make a good basket.

Other Fellow   (Hazard 1946) Single. Tube and sepals white; corolla pink with white shading at base. Small compact flowers. Upright growth. Flowers freely over a long period. Very attractive.

Pacquesa   (Clyne 1974) Single. Reflexing sepals deep red with crepe reverse; corolla pure white with faint trace of deep red veining. An excellent variety. Parentage Pacific Queen × Sheryl Ann (hence its name).

Papoose   (Reedstrom 1960) Single. Tube and sepals scarlet; corolla very dark purple but lighter at the base. Small compact blooms. The bushy self branching growth can be rather lax. Free-flowering.

Pee Wee Rose   (Neiderholzer 1939) Single. Tube and sepals rose; corolla deep pink. The flowers are quite small and borne in clusters on long willowy stems. Very vigorous growth in ideal conditions.

Phyllis★   (Brown 1938) Semi-double. Tube and sepals rose; corolla rosy red. Very floriferous, with a strong growth that can be trained to all shapes, with the exception of the basket. Height 3 feet (90 cm).

Pink Darling   (Machado 1961) Single. Tube dark pink; sepals pale pink; corolla soft lilac pink. Small flowers are held semi-erect.

Pink Galore   (Fuchsia La 1961) Double. Tube and upturned sepals candy pink; corolla a lighter shade of candy pink

Dark green glossy foliage. A natural trailer which will make an excellent basket. Very eye-catching when in full bloom.

Pink Marshmallow (Stubbs 1971) Double. Tube and sepals pale pink; corolla white with pink veining. Very large, open, loose-petalled blooms. Light green foliage. Natural trailer. Free-flowering and excellent in full or half baskets.

Pink Pearl (Bright 1919) Double. Tube and sepals pale pink; corolla deeper rose pink. Medium-sized blooms. Vigorous upright growth. Very floriferous.

Pixie* (Russell 1960) Single. Tube and sepals carmine red; corolla violet then blue-mauve. Light green foliage. Strong, self branching growth. This superb cultivar is a sport from Graf Witte. Height 3 feet (90cm).

Plenty (Gadsby 1974) Single. Thick tube carmine; sepals neyron rose; corolla violet purple. Excellent for all types of show work.

Postiljon (Van der Post 1975) Single. Tube white flushed pink; sepals creamy white, flushed rose pink with green tips; corolla rosy purple, white at base of petals. Compact grower, with small blooms freely produced. Very early flowerer which will make a good basket.

President Margaret Slater (Taylor 1973) Single. Long slender white tube; sepals white with a distinct pink flush and green tips; corolla mauve pink overlaid with salmon pink. Longish, medium-sized compact bloom. Foliage light green with serrated edge. Vigorous, free flowering, natural trailer. Makes an excellent basket or half basket. Flowers rather late in the season.

President Stanley Wilson (Thorne 1969) Single to semi-double. Carmine tube is long and slender; sepals carmine with green tips; corolla rosy carmine. Long compact medium-sized blooms. A natural trailer, and will make an excellent basket, as the flowers are held on long stems.

Princessita (Niederholzer 1940) Single. Tube white; sepals white with faint flush of pink on the underside; corolla very dark rose pink. Medium-sized blooms. Growth trailing. Vigorous and free-flowering.

F. procumbens (New Zealand) A ground hugging plant with small yellow flowers in which the purple sepals are completely reflexed. There is no corolla. Following the flowers are the seed pods which resemble miniature damson plums. These are much larger than the flowers and are a very attractive feature. The foliage consists of small round leaves. This plant is a hardy and would be ideal on a rockery. The seed pods should be left on the plant if exhibited at shows. The seeds can be collected and planted, and will come true to form.

Ravensbarrow (Thornley 1972) Single. Tube and sepals red; corolla very dark, almost black at first, fading slightly as the bloom matures. Dark green foliage. Free-flowering, bushy and vigorous. Eye-catching on the show bench.

Reading Show (Wilson 1967) Double. Short red tube; sepals red; corolla deep blue. Medium-sized blooms but floriferous for a hardy double. A good show plant.

Rose of Castille★ (Banks 1869) Single. Sepals waxy white; corolla purple faintly flushed rose, whitish at base. Very free-flowering and most attractive. Strong grower which can be used for most methods of training. Height 2 feet 6 inches (75 cm).

Royal Velvet (Waltz 1962) Double. Tube and upturned sepals crimson red; corolla luminous deep purple. An excellent variety which is good for the show bench.

Roy Walker (Walker – Fuchsia La 1975) Double. Small to medium-sized blooms with reflexed white sepals tinged with the palest of pinks; corolla white. Blooms remain in good condition for a long time. Good strong upright grower. Exhibition-type plant.

Rufus (the Red)★ (Nelson 1952) Single. Sepals and corolla a bright turkey red. Good strong growth and always in bloom. Although its correct name is Rufus, it is universally known as Rufus the Red. Excellent for all types of growth. Height 3 feet (90 cm).

Sandboy (Hall – Atkinson 1967) Single. Short thin tube. Sepals a very deep pink; corolla very deep mauve. Smallish flowers but blooms prolifically.

Shady Blue (Gadsby 1971) Single. Tube and sepals carmine pink; corolla violet blue shaded with pink at base of petals. Flowers are large and of good substance. Very free-flowering, upright self branching bush.

Shy Lady (Waltz 1955) Double. Tube and sepals white with the faintest touch of pink, on the outer petals. Dark green foliage. Upright, bushy, free-flowering plant.

Snowcap★ (Henderson) Semi-double. Sepals bright red; corolla pure white slightly veined with cerise. Very free-flowering. Can be used for all types of growth except basket. Not on the British Fuchsia Society Hardy List, but is considered to be hardy in most areas. One of the best, and should be in every collection. Height 2 feet 6 inches (75 cm).

Son of Thumb★ (Gubler 1978) Single. Sepals cerise; corolla lilac. Flowers small but very floriferous. A sport from Tom Thumb which is of similar growth. Height 12–18 inches (30–45 cm).

Sophisticated Lady (Martin 1964) Double. Tube and sepals soft pink; corolla white. The long pointed sepals extend well over the petals. A natural trailer which makes a very eye-catching basket.

F. splendens (syn. *F. cordifolia*) (Mexico) Tube red and long; sepals scarlet with green tips; corolla yellow green. An excellent species for the collector.

Stanley Cash (Pennisi 1970) Double. Tube white; sepals white with green tips; corolla deep royal purple. Medium-sized flowers. A trailer which is fairly vigorous in growth and free-flowering. A very attractive bloom which holds its shape well over a long period. Makes an eye-catching basket.

Swingtime (Tiret 1950) Double. Tube and sepals scarlet; corolla pure white with scarlet veining. Very full bloom. Its upright growth can be rather lax, and thus it is often used as a basket variety. It is vigorous and floriferous. Branches can be a little stiff at times for basket work, but with the aid of weights become more amenable. A really excellent variety.

Taddle (Gubler 1974) Single. Very short tube deep rose pink. The sepals are fully reflexed, hiding the tube when mature, and are also rose pink. The corolla is waxy white with slight pink veining. Light green foliage. Good bushy plant. Very floriferous.

Tennessee Waltz★ (Walker – Jones 1951) Semi-double to double. Sepals rose madder; corolla lilac lavender splashed with rose. Very large flowers continuously produced. An excellent variety suitable for training to other shapes. Height 2 feet 6 inches (75 cm).

Thalia (Turner 1855) *Triphylla*-type flower. Long tubular single flowers borne in clusters, orange scarlet in colour. Bronze green foliage. Excellent for outdoor bedding in the summer, with its foliage and flowers. Needs winter protection.

Ting a Ling (Schnabel 1959) Single. White self coloured. Extremely attractive form to the flowers which are produced in quantity. Strong upright grower, but needs to be kept from the sun to maintain a good white colour.

Tom Knights (Goulding 1983) Single. Short white to flesh-coloured tube; Sepals white shading to flesh; corolla lavender.

Tom Thumb★ (Baudinat 1850) Tube and sepals carmine;

corolla mauve veined carmine. Freely produced small flowers. Dwarf growing – ideal for the front of a border. Has produced sports Lady Thumb and Son of Thumb. Height 12–18 inches (30–45 cm).

Tom West (Meillez 1853) Single. Tube and sepals red; corolla purple, small and compact. Attractive foliage variegated pale greyish green and cream, with medium-sized leaves. Fairly vigorous growth rather lax. Does well in ornamental classes.

Trail Blazer (Reiter 1951) Double. Tube and sepals magenta; corolla deep magenta then rose purple. Long flowers very attractive. Natural trailer so will make a good basket.

Trase★ (Dawson) semi-double to double. Tube and sepals carmine red; corolla white with red veins. Short jointed growth. Free-flowering neat bush. Height 18 inches (45 cm).

Tsjiep (de Graaf 1983) Single. Long creamy white tube; sepals white on top, slightly flushed pink beneath; corolla orangey red. Very small flowers but very attractive. Ideal for small pot culture.

Vanessa Jackson (Handley 1980) Single. Tube and sepals salmon; corolla salmon orange. Large bloom, very floriferous for its size. Trailer – will make an excellent basket.

Walsingham (Clitheroe 1979) Semi-double. Tube and sepals off-white; corolla pale lilac with serrated edge. Growth upright and self branching. Attractive.

Westminster Chimes (Clyne 1976) Semi-double. Sepals rose; corolla violet blue. Smallish flowers but very profuse. Growth cascades quite naturally – ideal for small pot culture.

White Joy (Burns 1980) Single. Tube, sepals and corolla white. Upright growth. Floriferous.

White Pixie★ (Saunders 1968 or Rawlins 1969) Tube and sepals red; corolla white. Short jointed growth, self branching. Leaves have a yellow cast. Sport from Pixie with identical growth. Height 2 feet (60cm).

White Spider (Haag 1951) Single. Tube white striped red; sepals white flushed pink, very long and twisting. Corolla white then pale pink. Natural trailer used mainly for baskets but can be trained to many shapes. A well grown weeping standard would be very eye-catching.

Winston Churchill (Garson 1942) Double. Sepals pink; corolla lavender blue. Medium-sized but prolific blooms. Will make an excellent show plant.

3

Cultivation

GREENHOUSES

Rows of beautifully groomed plants on the show bench seem to suggest that a greenhouse is essential for the successful cultivation of fuchsias. And yet it is possible to grow fuchsias in practically any situation. No great expense is necessary to be able to produce an excellent display – in fact many keen growers simply have their plants in the garden, in tubs on the patio, in window boxes, in hanging baskets or in any available space. Even so, a greenhouse will add a further dimension to the number and type of plants that you can grow.

A study of any gardening periodical will show you a vast array of greenhouse structures, varying from a very small lean-to which can be attached to an available wall, to massive houses which would grace the garden of a stately mansion. The choice of greenhouse will therefore depend on the space available, and the materials used to build it.

Space

Careful consideration of the amount of space to be allocated to a greenhouse is important if it is not to overshadow the rest of the garden. But it is also important to try to purchase as large a greenhouse as possible at the outset – there is an old saying that, no matter how big the greenhouse you buy, you will soon require one even larger.

The actual positioning of the greenhouse is perhaps not quite so important, although there are arguments for and against siting it so that the longest sides are east to west or north to south. It should not be placed so close to large trees that it is shaded from the sun for long periods of the day – the debris falling from such trees can also be a nuisance. The ideal site, then, is one which is fairly open, yet protected from strong winds and not too far from the house. This last point is important when using a greenhouse to its full capacity, as means of heating and watering may then be needed. The greenhouse will be most in use in the cold, dark winter months when work outside is not possible. Access to the greenhouse by a well-lit, firm, dry path is therefore essential.

Make sure you allow enough space to be able to walk around the outside of the completed greenhouse. There is nothing more frustrating than not being able to get comfortably to one side or end of the house, because of a protruding fence or wall, when the inevitable happens and a pane of glass needs replacing. It has become common practice over the years to site a greenhouse towards the bottom of the garden but it is far more sensible to position your new structure as near to the house as possible.

It is also necessary, even at this time, to consider the possibility of further structures in the future – cold frames will probably be needed and the positioning of these could well come into your original reckoning. It is also wise to take into account the present position of smaller structures, such as clothes lines.

Materials

The most important considerations here are durability and expense. Three main methods of constructing greenhouses are common, using timber and glass, metal and glass, or metal or timber and plastic.

Plastic

The plastic-covered greenhouse has the shortest life span and is therefore by far the cheapest. There are a number of such houses on the market, which vary considerably in size and cost, but are nevertheless perfectly adequate to suit the needs of any particular gardener. Unfortunately, the plastic covering may only last for as little as three years.

There are several shapes available but the most common type is the plastic tunnel. These are used with great effect by large-scale market gardeners who think highly of them. One major benefit of this type of structure is that the cover can be replaced reasonably cheaply and with a minimum of effort as soon as it becomes inadequate. One disadvantage is that they will maintain a fairly high level of humidity, so it is often necessary to encourage greater air circulation by opening the doors at the ends. This will cause some heat loss in the early part of the season, and the advantages of having a greenhouse, to bring on earlier plants, will have been lost.

Other plastic-covered greenhouses are made in the

traditional shape with straight sides and sloping roofs. These usually have a framework of aluminium struts, are very sturdy, and have a rather more pleasing appearance than the tunnel shapes. It is also easier in this shape of greenhouse to erect staging for the presentation of your plants. Ventilation and heat loss are controlled through simple vents in the roof. This type of house is recommended for beginners' experiments with fuchsias, but it will probably be necessary to buy a more permanent structure within a short space of time.

Timber versus Metal

A timber or metal frame may be used to support the glass panels of a permanent greenhouse. Comparison of cost shows that the wooden houses are more expensive, but they are often preferred because of their more pleasing appearance. The type and colour of wood used may vary considerably. Soft timber houses look best painted white but will require regular maintenance to protect the woodwork and to keep their attractiveness. Red cedar houses are more expensive, but will need less maintenance – although fairly regular applications of a cedar preservative will enhance their colouring. Metal houses on the other hand are virtually maintenance free once erected.

The glazing bars of timber structures are wider than their metal counterparts, which will give added strength, but also cause a certain loss of light transmission. This loss, however, will be minimal and, where fuchsias are concerned, of little importance. Timber glazing bars will make insulation easier, and help to reduce the cost of heating the greenhouse during the cold winter months. A lining of plastic or bubble film reduces the heat loss through the glass, and, with a timber structure, this insulating material can be pinned directly into the woodwork. Although it is relatively simple to insulate a metal house using the same material, the special glazing clips needed do add to the cost of this operation. Similarly, timber frames are ideal to take hooks for hanging smaller baskets and pots. Although exact figures are not available, it is generally agreed that the heat loss from a timber house is less than that from a metal structure.

The shape of a permanent greenhouse may also vary, having straight or sloping sides. My own preference is for a house with traditional straight sides, as the provision of staging in this type is slightly easier.

With timber houses it is better to have glass to ground

rather than half-timbered sides, to give maximum flexibility in the positioning of staging for the plants, and to provide enough light below the staging to grow plants at ground level. My own preference is for glass to ground structures, although heat loss from these will tend to be greater. The main argument in favour of the sloping-sided greenhouse is that, especially as the majority are glass to ground types of houses, there is a greater area which can be used with good lighting.

Making the Choice

Your final decision will be determined by the factors of space, cost and convenience, but it is important always to take your time before choosing. Visit as many greenhouses owned by other enthusiasts as you can and find out the pros and cons of their structures. Discover if they are completely satisfied with their purchases or whether they would have made a different choice if given the opportunity. Send off for as many catalogues as you can – compare cost, ease of erection and speed of delivery.

If your final selection is made because of a recommendation please say so, as such recommendations are welcomed by manufacturers. Never be afraid to complain about poor service. If when you have completed the structure, it is not of the quality you expected or is not as accurate as you would hope, then say so. Manufacturers will bend over backwards to keep customers happy, and many are able to offer an erection service. If you are not particularly adept yourself or would have difficulty in getting assistance from friends or neighbours, this is well worth consideration – enquire at the time of purchase.

The foundations need to be prepared, very thoroughly, well in advance of the delivery of the house. As soon as the order has been finalised then the preparation can commence. The ground must be perfectly level, or you will run into difficulties as soon as the pieces of the house are bolted together. A concrete foundation for the walls is imperative, although a number of manufacturers supply substantial concrete blocks upon which the houses are fixed. Others provide metal foundations. Whichever type you choose, a solid foundation is essential for a satisfactory conclusion to the building of your greenhouse.

The best time of the year to purchase a new greenhouse is

probably in the autumn or early winter – when there is the least amount of work to do in the greenhouse. Early spring is likely to be a frustrating time as you may be anxious to start work in the house before it is completely ready. When the building work is over, the task of furnishing the empty shell begins.

Interiors

Before choosing the furniture for the greenhouse, a pathway must be constructed, to provide a good firm dry platform from which to tend the plants. The width of this will depend greatly upon the overall width of your house, but a minimum of two feet is perhaps the best advice that can be given. It is amazing how much space even the slimmest people need in which to turn from one bench to another when carrying a heavy tray of plants. This pathway can be of a permanent nature, made of concrete, or a semi permanent one, made from paving slabs. Slabs should be laid on a bed of sand so that they are level and firm.

The staging you will need for your plants must be carefully selected. It is important to consider the height of the staging from ground level, the provision of shelving towards the roof of the house, whether a space should be left in the staging so that taller structures may stand on the earth, and whether an area should be set aside for use as a propagating area. Plan out your staging very carefully indeed – timber or metal staging is not cheap and any mistakes made now are likely to be expensive ones.

Look again at the catalogues and see what is being offered – compare the cost of buying ready-made and made to measure staging, with what it would cost to construct your own. Timber and time can be expensive, but this time and effort might be compensated by having custom-built staging exactly where and how you want it. Again, look at the structures and staging used by others, which you may like to adopt, with personal amendments and improvements.

At this stage, you may also consider partitioning off part of the greenhouse, if it is a fairly large structure, with a view to maintaining different temperature levels. This might not appear to be important in the early part of the year, but in autumn and winter the need to keep the cost of heating within reasonable bounds is a vital factor. It is much easier to erect such a partition before positioning the staging.

Heating

The type of heating for your greenhouse needs careful consideration. A greenhouse which is not heated at all has its uses but its value is enhanced many times if the temperature inside can be raised. Fuchsias require heat to survive the winter, and even more is needed to keep them growing steadily. There are basically four types of fuel that need to be considered – five if one takes into account solid fuel boilers: mains gas; bottled gas; electricity and paraffin. I have not attempted to put them in any order of preference, neither will I attempt to compare costs. What needs to be considered, however, is their convenience and ease of use.

Mains Gas

Mains gas provides an easy, well controlled source of heat, but its disadvantage is that it has to be laid on to the greenhouse by means of piping, a process which must be done by a professional. Gas heaters are reasonably priced and have the benefit of being thermostatically controllable, which helps to conserve fuel. There is also no need to worry about running out of fuel. One fault is that once fixed they are permanently in position and are not mobile.

Bottled Gas

Bottled gas is a very useful commodity. The heaters are of comparable price to the mains gas variety and also have the advantage of being thermostatically controlled. One anxiety is that the gas cylinder will run out of gas at a crucial time – usually in the middle of the coldest night. An accurate gauge to measure the quantity of gas left in the cylinder would be a very useful implement but is not, to the best of my knowledge, yet available. The main disadvantage of this type of heating is the necessity to arrange for the delivery of full bottles and the changing from the empty to the full. They are, however, fairly portable and are relatively economic depending upon the temperature you wish to maintain. This is an ideal method of heating as a back-up system in a greenhouse when other heaters are being used.

Electricity

Electric heaters are perhaps the most expensive to use although it is possible to use the white meter tariffs if you have storage type heaters. The major advantages of electricity are that it is easy to control, can be used to heat at a thermostatically controlled level, and that it can be used to cool as well as heat. Disadvantages are that a supply of electricity needs to be laid on professionally to the greenhouse and power cuts would leave you completely without heating. There is a good choice of types of heater available on the market, most of which rely on a heater and fan to circulate the warm or cool air. The warmth obtained from electricity is a dry warmth which is certainly of considerable benefit in the cold damp months.

Paraffin

Paraffin heaters are usually the first type of heater that most growers try. The cost of the fuel is not particularly cheap, although it is comparable with all other types of fuel. Its disadvantages include the necessity of keeping a supply of paraffin, topping up the heaters, ensuring that the wicks of the heaters are always clean and that the flame is burning cleanly, that there is sufficient ventilation to ensure steady burning, and the excessive moisture produced when paraffin is burnt. The most important disadvantage is that paraffin heaters are not thermostatically controllable – they are either on or they are off. This can be frustrating if the heater is burning at full power on one of those balmy days in winter which start cold but then, with clear skies and the sun shining through the glass of the greenhouse, the temperature inside is raised considerably. This is no problem to those who are able to adjust their heating during the day, but it is very frustrating to those who cannot. The advantages of the paraffin heater are that it is portable, relatively cheap and there is no need for permanent piping or cables.

At the risk of repetition, it is important to compare all the factors mentioned. Send for catalogues or look at advertisements. Visit other growers and then make up your own mind.

Lighting

This might not be considered as important as heating, but if you are going to the expense of laying on power to your greenhouse, then in addition to plugs for the fan heaters it will be useful to have additional sockets for lighting. Even during daylight, in the depths of winter it is useful to have additional light when you are working on your plants. An added sophistication which you might well consider at a later date is the possibility of having 'sunlighting' so that additional hours of 'daylight' can be given to your plants to fool them into thinking that the longer summer days have arrived. If you wish to have very early flowering fuchsias then this type of lighting is a must. Very little research has been done on the length of day requirements of fuchsias so it is not possible to suggest any factual data to help you. Experimentation might well bring forward information that will be useful to others.

Propagating Boxes

The electric cables in your greenhouse will also be very useful if you plan to use propagating cases. It is possible to purchase electrically heated propagators quite cheaply. They vary in size from single seed tray size to double and four seed tray size. It is also possible to purchase complete propagating units. However, to make your own is not beyond the capabilities of even the most amateur carpenter.

The unit is quite simply a box shape that will fit satisfactorily on your greenhouse staging. The box consists of sides only as a sheet of thick black polythene is used as the base. The sides of the box need to be approximately 10 inches (25cm) high and I would suggest that they are made with half-inch planed timber.

The heating elements are under-soil cables and are readily available. A look at an advertisement will indicate the length of these cables and the area that they will heat, for example; 20 feet (6m) of cable will heat 6 square feet; 40 feet (12m) of cable will heat 12 square feet; 80 feet (24m) of cable will heat 24 square feet. So the dimensions of your box will look like this: given a width of 2 feet (60cm), you will need a box length of 3 feet (1m), 6 feet (2m) or 12 feet (4m) respectively, to fit the three lengths of cable. In addition to the cable it might be considered essential to invest in an adjustable thermostat. This will ensure that when the cables have warmed the sand bed to the required temperature, no more electricity will be used until the temperature drops below that level.

The cables are laid on a bed of sharp sand which is usually a couple of inches (about 5cm) in depth, although this is not critical. It is easier to lay the cables if they are warm as they are somewhat inflexible when cold. The cables should be laid carefully, according to the instructions given, and then covered with sharp sand to a further level of 2 inches (5cm). So you have a sandwich of sand, cables and sand.

The cables are attached to the thermostat which has a rod resting in the sand above the cable. When electricity is passed through the cables a warning light on the control box will glow and when the required temperature is reached, this light will be extinguished. Most boxes also have a warning light to show that power is reaching the box. To assist the conduction of heat it is necessary to maintain a moistness in the sand base of the propagating box.

Once our propagating box is ready for use, the only addition that might be considered necessary would be a cover. This can be made of glass or polythene to your own specifications and measurements. The longest propogating boxes will need to have a number of individual covers along their lengths.

Ventilation

Good ventilation is essential if your greenhouse is to function efficiently – plants enjoy the warmth, but hot stagnant air would be a killer. Automatic ventilators would therefore be very useful if it is not possible to be in attendance throughout the day. With a wooden greenhouse, these are very easy to install. Metal houses might pose slightly more of a problem, but nothing that cannot be easily overcome by most gardeners. Some greenhouses have ventilators low down on the sides. These are extremely useful and certainly help to circulate the air.

Shade

On very hot summer days, the fuchsias will need a certain amount of shading, as they will not tolerate very hot sun shining directly through the glass. This can be accomplished by painting the outer glass with a material which can be wiped off at the end of the season, but a more sophisticated and attractive method is to provide blinds that can be raised or lowered according to the weather conditions. Again, a wooden greenhouse will help when this type of fixing is necessary.

COMPOSTS

On one occasion I got into serious trouble with a fellow member of the BFS Committee by suggesting that the composition of any compost was unimportant, as it was purely a medium into which the plant could anchor its roots and that any nutrient required for the plant could be added when needed. I admit that this is an oversimplification and that it is of course important that the plant should receive a good balanced diet from the compost.

In order to provide the correct compost, it helps to establish the sort of environment fuchsias like to grow in. They require warmth and moisture, and they also insist that the compost should be well drained as they dislike sitting with their roots in water. So the compost must retain a certain amount of moisture and yet should be sufficiently well drained, so that air is available at the roots. Add to that the basic nutrients necessary for good strong growth, and the compost will be suitable for fuchsias.

I am often asked to recommend a compost for fuchsias, and I usually reply by asking a series of questions in return: What kind of compost do you like using for other plants that you grow? Do you use John Innes? If you do and can guarantee to get a good fresh supply, and have good success with it, then use it for your fuchsias. Do you use any of the numerous peat-based composts? If you do and are happy with the results you achieve, then use them for your fuchsias. Do you mix your own composts by buying either ready-made packs of compost mix or by purchasing all the individual chemicals and mixing your own? If you have success and satisfaction from so doing, then continue to do so. Do you get reasonable results from using soil from your own garden? If you do and are satisfied that your results are unlikely to be improved, then continue to use it.

The real answer is that the choice of compost must be a *personal* choice. After a time the grower will go by the *feel* of the compost – if it feels right then it is right, but this skill will come only with experience. My personal choice of compost is the peat-based Humber potting compost. I use this type of compost for all aspects of my growing, from the early cutting stage to mature plants. I like it in preference to other peat-based composts because it contains a greater percentage of sharp sand or small grit and as a result there is extra weight and support for the plants. The major criticism that some growers have of peat-based composts is that there is insufficient weight in the pot and that full grown plants can become top heavy. Humber does overcome this problem to a certain extent.

Another complaint against peat-based composts is that they tend to dry out very rapidly and are extremely difficult to remoisten. With the drying out of the compost there is a shrinkage away from the edge of the pot – when water is added, instead of remoistening the compost, it escapes down the side of the compost and the root ball remains dry. A wetting material has now been added to many of the newer peat-based composts which helps to alleviate this problem. However, I prefer to add my own cure and mix my compost with additional perlite or vermiculite. These two substances have the ability to absorb their own volume in water so, when water is added to the dry compost, a good quantity is absorbed by the perlite and will, in time, percolate into the peat base of the compost. The perlite thus has two opposing functions: to open out the compost and help with drainage, and to retain some moisture and keep the compost moist.

Mixing your own compost can certainly be a worthwhile exercise and can give excellent results. I would always recommend using the compost mixes available from such people as Chempak. These are good, nutritionally well-balanced compost mixes and the method of preparing them is simplicity itself. The basic requirements will be a quantity of peat and something with which the compost can be 'opened' for good drainage. The choice of drainage material is sharp sand, coarse silver sand if you can afford it, perlite or vermiculite. There is also some argument as to the type of peat that should be used – sphagnum moss peat or sedge peat. At one stage I would have strongly favoured the use of sphagnum moss as the only association I had had with sedge peat was when I had purchased a bag of very wet soggy material. Since then I have found that the sedge peat you can buy at DIY centres and garden centres is of a much drier and finer consistency. Again, the choice is simply a matter of personal preference. How to mix? Follow the instructions on the packet.

It is important to make sure that the compost is fresh. It is difficult to know precisely how long a compost will remain suitable for use once it has been mixed. There is bound to be a certain build up of chemicals within a sealed bag, which could be detrimental to the plants. It is a well-known fact that the loam-based John Innes composts need to be used quite quickly after mixing – but the problem is we cannot tell for sure when that mixing took place and how long the compost has been stored in the garden centre. Peat-based composts do not seem to suffer in the same way, although I prefer to obtain fresh supplies as often as I can. It might be a very useful aid to gardeners if manufacturers (or mixers) of compost were obliged to state the date of mixing on the packaging.

One important factor regarding peat-based composts should not be overlooked. The recommendation is always made on the bags not to overfirm the compost when potting. The suggestion is that the compost should be lightly trickled around the plant and then firmed purely by watering with a fine-rosed watering can thus settling the compost around the plant. Many other writers talk about gently firming with the fingers (never thumbs), but I would suggest that even this light firming should never be done when growing fuchsias. The act of firming causes the fibres of the peat to matt together, making drainage difficult. Get used to handling the compost – let it trickle through your fingers; get as much air into it as you possibly can before using it; get to know, and like, the feel of good compost, so that you can say, 'It feels right so it must be right'.

Pots – Clay versus Plastic

As with most aspects of horticulture, there is considerable discussion regarding the merits of using clay pots as opposed to plastic pots. Leaving aside the fact that plastic pots are so much cheaper and easier to obtain than clay pots, it is important to choose a pot which best suits your plants. Plants need to be able to breathe at the roots therefore an open compost is necessary. A porous clay pot lets that air penetrate through the pot into the compost, which is a great advantage. However, the moisture content of the compost is likely to be reduced more rapidly as a result of capillary action through the pot. So plants growing in clay pots will require a greater amount of watering, but are likely to flourish because of the additional air content of the compost.

Non-porous plastic pots will require less watering, in fact greater attention to the watering will be necessary to ensure that the compost does not become too soggy. With clay pots it is possible to discover if the plant is in need of watering by tapping the pot – a dry, ringing sound indicating that watering is necessary. With plastic pots such a test is not possible.

Plastic pots are much lighter, easier to handle, and stack far more easily. They are less likely to break, although in extreme frosty weather the plastic does become brittle and could split. Lifting clay pots by the rim is an easy method of transportation, whereas lifting a compost-filled plastic pot by the rim is fraught with danger. The heaviness of the clay pot gives it greater stability and even when it contains a very large plant, the weight of the pot plus the compost is usually sufficient to keep it upright. Plastic pots, however, are liable to be unstable, especially when used with peat-based composts.

Looking at the pot and the compost together, it would be fair to say that clay pots and peat-based composts are not really suitable for each other, as the moisture content of the peat is absorbed by the porosity of the pot. Conversely, the heavier loam-based composts, when used in plastic pots, often remain too moist too long and result in the demise of the root system.

The final choice is once again a matter of personal preference. Peat-based composts are better if used with plastic pots; Loam-based composts are better used in conjunction with clay pots. In the final analysis it is possible that lightness, cheapness, ease of cleaning and availability will win the day and plastic pots will emerge the winners.

Complaints are occasionally received from those who have purchased rooted cuttings growing in peat pots from nurserymen. The complaint centres on the fact that the roots have difficulty in penetrating the walls of the peat pots as the manufacturers claim that they should. Many purchasers try to overcome this difficulty by trying to remove the peat pot itself, only to find that many young white roots are damaged in the process. Personally, I have never found any great difficulty with them and have purchased many plants grown in such containers over the years.

The recommendation of the manufacturers is that, prior to using the pots, they should be thoroughly soaked for a number of hours. When purchasing plants I continue the process before potting on into other pots and leave the peat pot soaking in water overnight. The whole of the pot is then sunk into the new compost contained in my own pot. Care is taken to ensure that the whole of the peat pot is below the surface of the fresh compost. This prevents the possibility of the top rim of the peat pot drying out – if it does so, it tends to leach the moisture from the remainder of the peat pot, causing it to become hard once again and preventing the roots from growing through the sides. Keeping the compost in the new pot rather moister than sometimes considered necessary prevents any possible losses due to drying out.

I do not root young fuchsia cuttings in this type of pot, but would not hesitate to purchase one if it were the type of cultivar I had been seeking. Such complaints are rarely made against cuttings rooted in Jiffy 7 type pots. It is possible to see the young roots growing through the mesh of the container, which has no restricting effect on the young plants.

NEW LIFE

At the beginning of February, when hopefully the severest part of the winter has passed, and we are looking forward to the break of spring, our plants will begin to reawaken from their winter sleep. If your plants are buried in the garden, or you are not in a position to give your plants adequate warmth from now onwards, delay the following process for at least another month, that is, until the beginning of March at the earliest.

Rested Plants

For those lucky enough to have heated greenhouses where the plants can be given extra special care, it is now time to think about the rejuvenation process. Mature plants, which have been allowed to rest completely during the winter, are probably looking a little sorry for themselves. If satisfactorily over-wintered, they will consist of a pot containing a very bare looking plant. The question we are now dying to see answered is whether the plant is still alive. My first suggestion will be rather an anticlimax to that question, as in the first instance you should leave the plant precisely where it is. The only action you need to take is to give the plant a very good syringeing, or spraying, with clear tepid water. When this has been completed the pot should be placed in the warmest position in the greenhouse. The action of spraying will immediately make the plant look livelier, as the wood will take on a brighter look. Each day, or perhaps even twice or three times a day, the plants should be given a good spraying. You will notice that I have not suggested watering the compost at this stage although a quantity of the water from the spray will have fallen on to the old compost, moistening it slightly. The object of this spraying is to soften up the wood of the branches and encourage the dormant shoots in the leaf axils to start to grow. It is very exciting when the first little pink buds appear in the axils as it is only then that you can be sure that your plants are alive.

Hopefully, such signs will be evident after a couple of weeks, and you can then move on to the next process, which is to completely renew the compost in the pots. I think it is important at this stage to have a really good compost, freshly made if possible, ready for use. Remove all the old compost from the root ball, first using a pointed stick to get in amongst the old roots and then finally by dipping the whole lot in a bucket of tepid water. Whilst clearing away the old compost keep an eye open for any vine weevil larvae that may be present. If there are any, destroy them with the aid of a large boot. These greyish white larvae, about a quarter of an inch long, do considerable damage to the young roots of the plant.

When the old compost has been removed, some fresh young white roots will be seen. It is also a good idea at this stage to remove any of the old gnarled roots that there may be, especially any damaged ones, using a sharp pair of secateurs.

Having reduced the size of the root ball quite considerably, repot the plant into a fresh, clean pot at least one size smaller than the pot from which the plant was removed. Put a quantity of the fresh compost in the bottom of the pot, place the plant on this compost and let fresh compost trickle around and between the roots until the pot has been filled. I find that gently lifting the plant every now and again whilst the compost is being trickled in ensures that there are no air gaps around the roots. Do not compress or firm the compost in any way but settle the compost by simply tapping the pot on the edge of your potting bench. The compost will have been slightly moist when used for this process so there will be no need at this stage to water the plant again.

Although the plant will have received quite a traumatic shock having had its roots pruned in this way, this is also a good time to carry out the pruning of the top growth. Remember that fuchsias do not flower on old wood but only on fresh new season growth. We therefore want as little old wood as possible to be left on the plant or we will have a plant with a long old stem and a considerable gap at the bottom without flowers. Pruning can thus be quite drastic.

Having already seen signs of fresh growth in the leaf axils, it is possible to see precisely how far back you must go to cut out the old wood. I would suggest that all branches should be shortened back until they are no more than 2 or 3 inches (5–7½cm) long. If, when your plant was originally formed, stops were made at an early stage so that branches formed quite close to the compost, you will see at this point how it is possible to cut your plants back quite severely and still maintain a good shape.

Having completed the potting back, root pruning, and branch pruning, the plants should again be placed in the best position possible for them – a warm spot in the greenhouse, as near to the light as possible. The treatment from now on will consist of a daily spraying of the upper framework with tepid water, to continue to encourage those dormant shoots to break. If the compost becomes dry then this should also be watered with a fine-rosed watering can – but do not let the compost become too saturated and make sure that the pots drain well. Within a couple of weeks you should see signs of good thick growth. These shoots will grow on steadily now and some of them could be removed for propagation purposes. It is important, however, if your intention is to keep a plant for the show bench, to take as few cuttings as possible and encourage the plant to build up a good skeleton of branches which will bear a great quantity of flowers for you later in the season.

Young Plants

The young plants which were not allowed to go to sleep in the winter but were kept growing steadily, albeit slowly, in a temperature of just over 40 degrees fahrenheit (5°C), will need very little treatment other than that which you would normally give a young growing plant. I would suggest that you remove each plant from its pot and examine the root ball. Tease away as much of the old compost as you possibly can (some people go to the extreme of washing away *all* the old compost) and repot the plant in the same sized pot. Generally speaking this will be a three and a half inch pot (9cm).

A gentle pruning, or shaping, of the branches at this time can be advantageous, the pruning really being no more than stopping each of the growing tips. However, make sure that each of the growing tips is removed so that growth from now on will be even. Again I would stress that the new compost should not be firmed around the roots with fingers or thumbs but that the only firming necessary will be a slight tap of the pot on the bench. Subsequent watering will firm the compost sufficiently. These plants will grow very quickly once the temperature and light intensity rise and will make excellent plants in larger pots later in the season.

Standards

Standards which have been overwintered in the greenhouse by lying them on their sides can be dealt with in a similar way. They should be repotted into fresh compost and the top growth should be cut back quite severely – back to two pairs of leaf nodes on each branch would be ideal to encourage a nice thick bushy head. Spray as regularly as possible to encourage shoots to break.

If there seems to be some delay in this process it might help if you lie the plant on the bench and spray regularly. This lying down of the plant often encourages the shoots to break. if the shooting is one-sided then turn the plant over so that the side not shooting is uppermost. The compost in the pots needs to be kept just moist to encourage those fresh young white roots to form. Unfortunately very often the new growth of standards is a little uneven and renders them unsuitable for show work but very suitable for ordinary display work in the garden.

Garden Plants

Plants that were left out in the garden will not show signs of growth from them for a little while yet. Do not be tempted, yet, to cut back the old dead-looking branches which have been giving that little extra protection through the frosts. Leave them in position until growth from the base of the plants is visible. Keep an eye on the base of the plants as the weeks go by and the air begins to warm. Towards the middle of March it is possible that fresh young shoots will be seen poking through the soil – if so, the plants will grow on steadily from now onwards.

If the winter has not been too severe, young growths might be seen on the old branches. Please don't be tempted to keep these growths but cut back all of your plants to about 2 or 3 inches (5–7½cm) from the ground. You do not really want bare stems for any height so it is important to encourage growths from the base of each plant. The fact that they have shown signs of growing higher up indicates that the plant is alive so no harm can come to it by cutting back very hard.

Buried Plants

If you were really brave and buried your plants in a grave in the garden then mid March might be an ideal time to consider exhuming them. Be careful how you dig them out and you will probably be surprised to see some very long straggly white growths from the branches. This is a very good sign because at least you know your plants are alive. The object now is to clean them up and to treat them in exactly the same way as those plants which were kept in a frost-free greenhouse or shed. Repot them in a smaller sized pot, root prune and top prune, then give them preferential treatment to encourage good young strong growth.

Young Cuttings

Cuttings may be taken (as explained later in this chapter), to ensure that plants which are being left in the garden continue to be part of your collection even if the severity of the winter kills the parent plant. If, as a result of growing these cuttings and, if necessary, having taken cuttings from the cuttings, your plants are ready to be moved on into larger pots, I would suggest that you proceed slowly. These cuttings will have been growing in an ideal mini-climate and to take them from these ideal conditions too rapidly would cause a rather severe shock. I would suggest that on the first day the propagator with its cuttings should be left in its position but the screw top (which is now the saucer) should be released so that some air is allowed into the jar. As the days progress, gradually allow more air into the jar until, after three or four days, the young plants will be sufficiently acclimatised and can be left completely without their cover protection. Gradually harden them off before removing them to their new home in the greenhouse.

Where the place used for this propagation method has been rather warm, many people have discovered that their young cuttings have collapsed on removal from the propagator. I think it is important to experiment with this type of propagation so that the young plants do not suffer too severely. If the plants have become too leggy then it might be a worthwhile exercise, at this juncture, to remove the soft growing tip and use this as a cutting. The plant from which this cutting has been taken can of course be grown on as a young plant, the removal of the cutting having served simply to stop the plant.

STOCKING UP

Spring is a very busy time of the year for gardeners every-where and I would strongly advise that you take stock of the materials that you will need during the coming season. There is nothing more frustrating than to start a task only to find that you do not have all the equipment necessary. The following is a short check-list of essential items.

Compost
Ensure that you have adequate supplies of fresh compost, or the materials with which you make your own. The majority of the peat-based composts have a very good shelf-life, so nothing is lost by buying in sufficient quantities in one go. (This might even prove to be a cheaper method of buying).

Pots
Make sure you have pots of all the various sizes that you will need. I love using new pots but if you are in the position of having to recycle pots that have been used in previous seasons, please ensure that they are well cleaned.

Labels and Marking Pens
Again, it is most frustrating to run out of labels so make sure that you have a good supply. Marking pens or pencils should be readily available and kept in a place where they are easily found. Marking pens, if the tops are left off, tend to dry out very quickly, so always replace the top after writing each label or group of labels. I find that an ordinary HB pencil is suitable for ordinary plastic labels and the writing lasts for a couple of seasons. (But keep an eye on them and replace if the writing begins to get a little faint).

Canes
Flower sticks of 18 inches (46cm) and 30 inches (76cm) will be needed during the growing season so get in a good selection now. For heavier work with standards, three feet and four feet canes will be needed. As they always seem to be in short supply when required, think early.

Insecticides and Fungicides
These will be covered more fully in a later section, but again it is a good idea to get in your initial supplies now.

You may also want to stock plants. From early in the year it is possible to obtain current catalogues from recognised fuchsia nurseries. Many pleasant hours can be spent just browsing through such lists. I feel that it is always best to visit the nursery from which you intend to purchase so that you can see the quality and select your own plants. If you have to depend upon a postal service try to use a nursery of which you have good reports and which specialises in this type of work. The packing of plants for postal delivery is an art, and success or failure depends upon the care taken.

Always try to order your new stock or visit a nursery as early as possible in the season. Failure to do so might easily mean that the stocks of the plants you require will have become exhausted. The correct naming of your new plants is important so always make sure that a label is firmly attached to the plant – there is nothing more frustrating than to arrive home and find that the labels have fallen off. It would perhaps be fair to say do not buy too many, but the temptation to do so will be there at the beginning of the season – and most of us will succumb to that temptation.

TAKING CUTTINGS

One of the nicest things about growing fuchsias is without doubt the fact that new plants are so easily produced by the simple process of removing pieces from the plant and rooting them. Once again, there are no set rules that you *must* follow but, there are certain guidelines which will help you towards success.

First of all – what is a cutting? Quite simply, it is any piece removed from a parent plant which is then encouraged to root. From this brief description it would appear that practically any piece of a plant, once removed, and given the right conditions will form new roots and thus form a new plant. There is an element of truth in this, but for our purposes it is better to say that the part of the fuchsia plant which will form roots most easily is what is often described as the soft green tip.

It is probably fair to say that if a plant were given to a dozen expert fuchsia growers with the instruction to take a cutting, we would probably have a dozen different types of cuttings. There are no set rules, no one way to take a cutting – success can be achieved with any of the methods used.

Types of Cuttings

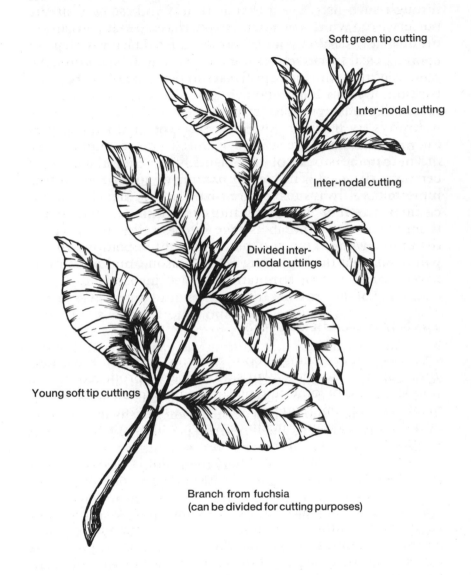

Soft green tip cutting

Inter-nodal cutting

Inter-nodal cutting

Divided inter-nodal cuttings

Young soft tip cuttings

Branch from fuchsia
(can be divided for cutting purposes)

There are many opinions as to whether a cutting should be removed from the plant by cutting just beneath the leaf node or by cutting above it. In most horticultural books the recommendation is to cut below the leaf node (that is, where the leaves join the stem) as this is the point at which the greatest hormonal activity is concentrated. The hormones are concentrated at the very tip of the stem and then gradually reduce in strength as they proceed down the stem just beneath the skin. When a leaf node is reached the hormones build up rather like a river arriving at lock gates. This build up of hormones means that greater rooting potential is present at the nodal position.

The principal is a sound one and it is a method that I certainly favour when dealing with cuttings that are rather more mature, consisting of semi-hard wood. But the soft tip cuttings are very immature and the hormones needed for them to root are stronger as they are nearer the tip. I would therefore recommend that you sever the cutting from the parent plant just *above* the leaf node. This means that you will have a small cutting approximately 1½ inches (4cm) long, consisting of the growing tip, a pair of immature leaves, a pair of slightly more mature leaves, and a short spur of stem about a quarter of an inch long. Many growers take longer cuttings but I do not consider that anything is gained by so doing.

Give the plant a good watering about twelve hours before removing the cutting, so that the whole plant, including the very tips of each of the shoots, is fully charged with moisture. The parent plant should be a good strong healthy one, typical of the cultivar chosen, and free from pests and diseases. It is a well known fact that like begets like, so a cutting from a good strong healthy plant is more likely to produce a healthier plant than one taken from a weak and unhealthy looking specimen.

The medium used to root the cuttings is an important consideration, and there is again considerable discussion as to whether the compost should contain any nutrient or not. Cuttings will root in any medium provided that it contains moisture and is warm and humid. Fuchsias cuttings will root in a glass of water, in moist sand, in moist peat, in moist perlite or vermiculite, in anything which will hold moisture.

The recommended cutting compost is 50:50 peat and sand. Given warmth the cuttings will root quite rapidly. The new roots will start their search for food, and, as none is available, more roots will be formed and the search for food will be intensified. An excellent root system will thus be formed very quickly indeed. As soon as sufficient rooting has taken place this type of rooted cutting must be potted on into a compost containing nutrient or it will rapidly become starved and rather woody. So, if you are able to pot on your cuttings as soon as they are ready then this method of rooting is recommended.

Most people, however, are not so lucky as to be able to carry out their gardening tasks when the plants most desire it and so I would recommend a variation of this method. The compost I prefer to use consists of 50:50 ordinary potting compost (Humber, in my case) and vermiculite. I use this because I now have a compost containing a dilution of normal nutrients and a soft material which opens out the compost and helps to keep it moist. I like my cutting compost to be soft, light and fluffy – I do not want any hard, coarse grains of sand as I do not wish to damage the base of the cutting once it has begun to root. I find that this type of compost does promote a good root system although this will not be quite as concentrated as that produced with the non-nutrient type.

You will probably have noticed that I have not mentioned using hormonal rooting powders. This is because I have found that with small, soft tip cuttings, there is no need, as rooting takes place very easily. But, if you are in the habit of using rooting powders for all your cuttings, please continue to do so. They do no harm and they might well do some good as they contain a fungicide which could help prevent damping off of the cuttings.

Having taken a cutting and chosen a compost, you will need to select a suitable container – again this is a matter of individual choice. An electrically heated propagator is also a good idea, as they often prove to be very successful. In fact if they have a fault it is that they are *too* successful in that they provide too much heat. Earlier in this chapter I mentioned that your cuttings will need some warmth. 'Warmth' is the important word. Too great a heat will cause the plants to either dry out, or become too soft and damp and rot off. So to get my warmth I usually put a layer of perlite in the base of the tray as slight insulation. As this will also absorb water it serves a dual purpose in that it maintains a high humidity in the tray. Within the tray I like to place a second tray which has sixty small compartments – such as the Plantpak 60 trays. I like my young rooted cuttings to have their own individual compartments as there will be less root disturbance later.

Compost is placed in the tray without any firming

whatsoever. The compost should be just moist and should be soft, light and fluffy. The cuttings can now be prepared and I would suggest using the cuttings from one plant at a time so that they do not become mixed. I like to take a strip across the tray (six) of each cultivar and then I can place just one label at the end of each line. When the cuttings have been prepared to the length I have suggested, they can be gently pushed into the compost so that the first pair of leaves just rests on the surface of the compost.

For those of you who have just held your hands up in horror at my comments that I 'push' the cutting into the compost, let me explain that it is my belief that a light airy compost such as mine cannot damage the tender end of the shoot. If a harsher compost is being used then certainly a hole made with a dibber before insertion of the cutting would be recommended. The reason often given for making a hole with a dibber first is so that when the cutting is placed in position the dibber can be used to gently firm the compost around the base of the cutting, ensuring that there are no air gaps left. My argument is that if I gently push the cutting into a soft compost there must be contact with the compost at the base of the cutting without any type of firming. Once a line of cuttings has been inserted, place the label in position. Do not leave it until later or your memory might well let you down and it is important that all cuttings should be correctly named.

Once the whole tray has been filled with cuttings water the tray through a fine rose. This will then cause the compost to settle around the cuttings. They are then ready for placing in a position where they can be left to root. I would suggest now that the best position would be where the tray will have light but not direct sunshine. If you are placing them in a greenhouse the propagator should be shaded from any sun that there might be by covering with a sheet or two of newspaper. Sun, even in early spring, shining through the glass of the greenhouse and through the cover of the propagator will cause a drying heat inside the box and the cuttings will shrivel away.

So, with shade from hot sun and the warmth from the heater in the base of the propagator, roots will have started to form within two or three weeks. There will be no need for you to have a little tug at the cuttings to see if they have rooted, they will tell you. When you look at an unrooted cutting it has a rather dull look about it but once it has rooted it takes on a brighter, glossy look. Even when rooted I prefer to leave the cuttings in these trays for another two weeks to form a good root system. By the end of that time the whole tray will be full, almost to overflowing, with fresh, green-looking young plants.

Once you are satisfied that all the cuttings have rooted you will need to pot them on into larger individual pots. At this stage I prefer to use either 2½ or 3 inch (6 or 7cm) square pots. I prefer square pots as they take up less room on the staging. The compost I use for this first potting is my usual Humber compost with a small proportion, approximately twenty per cent of perlite added for drainage purposes. They are left in these smallish pots until they tell me they are ready to move on into larger pots, having filled their pots with roots.

It is quite possible that you will not require as many cuttings as I have suggested. If so, you can use a small propagator, perhaps a half tray size with a perspex top, or a 3½ inch (9cm) pot with a perspex top, or anything which will help you to keep a moist atmosphere around the cuttings. Old plastic sweet jars are ideal for this purpose, as are cut down plastic lemonade bottles.

One of the simplest and yet most effective propagators is a coffee jar. The large-sized jars are ideal in that they can hold a two inch pot quite easily. Firstly remove the cardboard disc from inside the lid of the jar. If this is left in position, with the moisture and warmth, mould soon forms which could be detrimental to the cuttings. The lid will now become the tray upon which the pot will stand. Fill the pot with compost (do not firm) and gently insert the cuttings – you can get three small cuttings in a 2 inch pot quite easily without them touching each other. Insert the label and then give a thorough watering with a fine-rose watering can. Place the pot on the lid and then screw on the glass jar, so that no air can get in or out.

This jar can then be placed on a windowsill in a cool room provided that the window does not face towards the sun. If it is essential to place the jar in a sunny window it will be necessary to provide some shade. The jar can remain in this position until the cuttings show signs of rooting. There will be no need to worry about watering as the moisture within the jar cannot escape and will be re-used when needed. As soon as there are signs of rooting, take a couple of days to allow your cuttings to get used to the outside world by unscrewing the lid gradually, and then pot on as already described.

This is just one variation on the theme of propagators –

Propagators

A jam jar inverted on top of the pot

An inverted coffee jar. A pot is placed on
the lid and the jar is screwed back on

A pot covered with a clear plastic bag,
sticks holding it out and secured by
elastic bands

A plastic sweet bottle cut in half,
planted and placed back together again

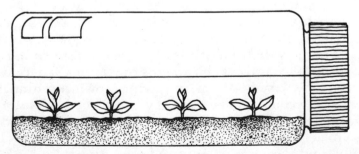

Simple propagator made with a plastic
lemonade bottle and polystyrene tray

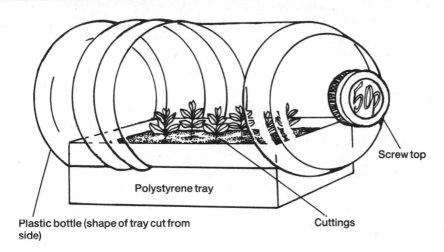

Screw top

Polystyrene tray

Plastic bottle (shape of tray cut from
side)

Cuttings

fertile imaginations will, I am sure, produce many other
methods of achieving the same aims.

So far I have only dealt with the very small soft tip cuttings
which are available in spring, but it is important to realise that
such cuttings are often available at other times of the year
when plants are making fresh growth. This is particularly
obvious in the autumn when plants seem to take on a fresh
lease of life and many new shoots are formed. A look at the
hardy plants growing in the garden in autumn will prove this
point. The soft, succulent, fresh green growth available then
is ideal for cutting material.

There are times, however, when it may be necessary to take
cuttings from plants when they are still producing flower
buds. Cuttings taken at this time will root, but a slightly
different approach is necessary. Such cuttings can be a little
larger, say 2½ to 3 inches (6–7½cm) in length, and will consist
of a growing tip and three pairs of leaves. Within the growing
tip it is possible that there will be young flower buds – these
should be carefully removed as they are likely to die and rot if
left in position.

The cutting should be trimmed just beneath the bottom
pair of leaves, which should themselves be removed. The next
pair of leaves can be reduced in size by about half. The base of
the moistened cutting should be dipped in a hormone rooting
powder and then inserted into the usual compost for cuttings.

The cuttings should be kept in a humid condition and should be shaded from the sun. As these cuttings are rather harder than the spring cuttings they will take a little longer to root, perhaps three to four weeks. I have mentioned using hormone rooting powder in this case – I only use this sort of aid for these half-ripe cuttings. Other people will still not find the need to use it, so it will simply be a matter of personal choice.

Occasionally we need to get a good supply of a certain cultivar as quickly as possible. If only the tips of branches are used as cuttings then the number of cuttings available will depend upon the number of branches that there are, but it is possible to gain additional cuttings quite easily. In the axil of every leaf there is a small bud, either in a dormant state, or in the course of developing. These buds can be used as cuttings.

The method is quite simple and consists of removing a pair of leaves from a branch by cutting across the stem just above and about a half an inch below the leaf node. This means that you will have a piece of stem about three quarters of an inch long from which two leaves are growing. Slice down through the centre of the stem with a sharp razor blade so that you now have a half piece of stem with a leaf protruding from it. These pieces can be treated as individual cuttings and will grow to form a fresh plant. As you can see, from just one branch it will be possible to produce perhaps a dozen or more cuttings.

It is not essential to slice the stem to produce two cuttings as the whole piece can be treated as one cutting if you prefer. If it is gently pushed into the compost it will, when rooted and growing, produce a young plant with two strong shoots coming up from beneath the compost: a good start for a shrub plant.

I hope that what I have written will encourage you to have a go at producing new plants of your own. Remember that each plant which you produce from cutting material will be an exact replica of the plant from which the cutting is taken.

SHAPING YOUR PLANTS

As soon as your cuttings have rooted, decide for what purpose you will be using them. There are several different types of growth and the type of plant and the vigour of the cutting will decide its ultimate destination: bush, shrub, standard, basket, fan, pillar, espalier, or pyramid. It would be fair to say that the majority of fuchsias are grown as bushes or shrubs. The British Fuchsia Society define a bush as a plant growing on a single stem no more than 1½ inches (3½cm) in length with numerous branches making a very bushy plant. A shrub is similar except that more than one growth is permitted from below soil level.

Bush

If a cutting were left to go its own way without any training whatsoever you would soon get a long spindly stem with very few side branches – it would grow somewhat similarly to a vine. So to ensure that a nice compact bushy plant is achieved, as soon as the cutting has rooted well it should be removed from the propagator and potted into its own individual pot – either a 2½ inch (6cm) square pot or a 3 inch (7½cm) round pot. As soon as it has become established in this pot – a matter of a couple of days – the training process can start and consists simply of removing the small growing tip from the plant. Remove the smallest portion that you can.

There is always discussion about the right sort of tool to use for this purpose, some use a razor blade, others the blade of a knife, others finger and thumb. I use none of these methods, as I wait until the growing tip is sufficiently large that it can be gently bent at right angles from its leaves until it snaps off. By doing it this way I know there will be no damage to the small shoots in the leaf axils and that it will snap off cleanly, especially if the plant was well watered an hour or so prior to this operation. With a little practice I am sure that you will find this to be a very satisfactory method.

Having removed the growing tip in this way it will be impossible for the plant to continue to grow upwards, so the vigour of the plant will have to go into the growth of the side shoots in the leaf axils. If there were two pairs of leaves when the stop was made then you will now have four growing tips coming from your plant. These shoots should be allowed to grow until they have each made two pairs of leaves and a growing tip, and then the growing tips should again be removed. This will result in four shoots from each of the four branches, so that the bushy plant now has sixteen branches. This might be considered enough and the plant could be allowed to grow on and flower.

One important point to remember is that when growing tips are removed from the branches of any plant *all* tips should

Training Bush Plants

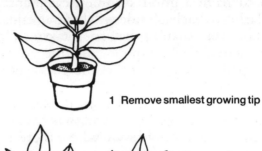

1 Remove smallest growing tip

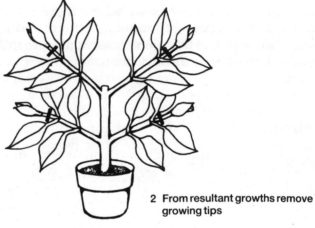

2 From resultant growths remove growing tips

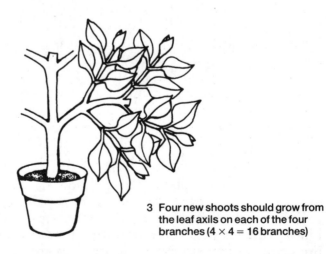

3 Four new shoots should grow from the leaf axils on each of the four branches (4 × 4 = 16 branches)

be removed at the same time. This will encourage even growth. During this growing process it is advisable, if you wish to have a good symmetrical plant, to turn the plant regularly so that each side will have an equal share of the light.

Whilst this shaping has been taking place the plants will have grown fairly rapidly and the root system will have developed to the extent that the pots will have become filled with roots. Never, in the training process, allow the pot to become root bound but increase the size of the pot by one inch to encourage further root, and thus top, growth. Remember that a plant will only grow where there is root movement – once the roots become stationary and the compost exhausted the plant will feel threatened and will start to form its flower buds. This is nature's way of ensuring the continuation of the species.

Shrub

The method of training for a shrub is very similar to that for a bush. You could, of course, start with a double-headed cutting, that is, one which consists of a piece of stem with a pair of leaves and the buds growing in the leaf axils. This will give you a head start as you will have two branches growing from below soil level. When they have grown two or three pairs of leaves each, remove the growing tips to encourage the formation of those side shoots. Then continue as with the bush, remembering to pot on as soon as the pot is filling with roots. When you have achieved the number of branches that you desire, the plant can be allowed to grow on and flower.

Most shows do not separate these two types of growth but specify bush or shrub trained. But remember if it does ask for a bush plant, there should be one stem only from the ground. (Any of the cultivars described in detail as recommended cultivars can be used for the growing of bushes and shrubs.)

Timing

I have mentioned several times that when you have achieved the number of branches you desire, the plant can be allowed to flower. The question often asked – which is a very important one if you are anxious to have plants in full flower for a certain date – is how long after the final pinching out of a branch will the plant take to flower? If you wish, you can keep on pinching out the growing tips and getting a bushier and bushier plant, but it will be all foliage and of little use for decorative purposes.

The time from the final pinching out of the growing tip to the production of the first flowers will vary according to whether the plant produces single or double flowers. If the plant is a single flowered variety then you will require a period of between six and eight weeks before your shoots will produce flowers. A double flowered variety requires a longer period of time – eight to ten weeks is average.

These times are only a very rough guide – it is necessary to know your varieties, as some will take much longer to flower. It is also important to realise that it will take about six weeks from the pinching out of the growing tip for the resultant shoot to reach the same stage of maturity. This means that if there were embryo buds in the shoots that you pinched out then in six weeks you will have shoots also bearing embryo buds. If you add two weeks on to that time for the development of the buds into flowers you can see that a period of eight weeks is needed. But if there were no buds in the shoots when they were finally pinched out then it is possible that a little longer time will be needed until we achieve the desired result.

Quarter Standards

The standard is, I think, one of the most satisfying shapes to try. There is nothing nicer than a well grown standard fuchsia in the centre of a bed of flowers giving that all important height. Although they take a little longer there is nothing particularly difficult about growing a standard.

I suggest that you start with either an autumn struck cutting or a very early spring one. The cutting you should choose for this purpose needs to be a strong growing one with a good straight stem. Pot the cutting on into a 3 inch (7½cm) pot and immediately place a flower stick alongside, gently securing the stem of the cutting to this stick. This will serve two purposes, the first to remind you that you must not remove the growing tip of this plant and the second to start the training of a nice straight stem. The stem should be tied to the stick between each pair of leaves so that no kinking of the stem will occur. Allow the stem to grow straight up the stick and remove any small side shoots that form, other than those side shoots in the top three sets of leaf axils.

This is a rather controversial point, as there is a strong band

Training standards

1 Remove side shoots
from leaf axils

2 Leave top three side
shoots as stem
develops

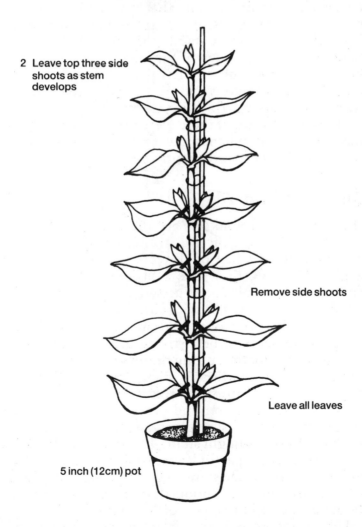

Remove side shoots

Leave all leaves

5 inch (12cm) pot

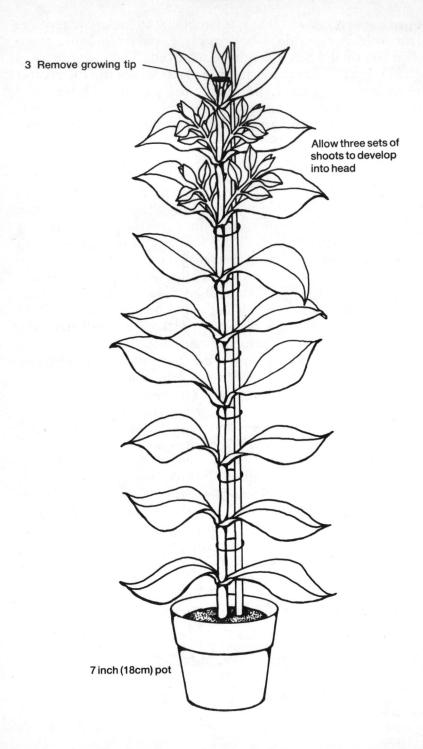

3 Remove growing tip

Allow three sets of
shoots to develop
into head

7 inch (18cm) pot

of growers who insist that it is beneficial to the growth of the plant to leave the side shoots in place, only removing them when the final desired height is achieved. Their argument is valid in that the plant takes in food via its leaves and the greater the quantity of leaves, the better the growth. However, I would insist that by leaving the leaves on the stem there is sufficient manufacture of the necessary elements by the plant. This is a vital point – under no circumstances should the leaves of the plant be removed until the required height has been reached and a head has been formed. My feeling about leaving the side shoots in place is that I would prefer to remove them at a very early stage by simply rubbing them out, rather than to risk scarring the trunk later on when larger side shoots would have to be cut away. I also feel that with all the strength and vigour of the plant concentrated on the one growing tip, there is bound to be faster upward growth. But this is a matter of opinion and either method will give success. If the top three sets of shoots are left in the leaf axils then, should anything happen to the growing tip of the plant, you will have the shoots from which a head can be formed.

The stem will grow upwards, beautifully straight and supported by a split stick. Keep an eye on the pot so that there is no possibility whatsoever of the pot becoming full of roots. As soon as the roots are seen on the surface of the compost, when the plant is removed from the pot, then it is time to pot on into the next sized pot. At no time should the plant be allowed to feel threatened or else it will start to produce flower buds and upward growth will slow down. The type of standard that you require will decide the length of stem. If you wish to grow a quarter standard (10–18 inches or 25–45cm clear stem) then allow your plant to grow to about 15 inches (38cm) and then remove the growing tip. Proportionally, we should be aiming for a head which is approximately one third of the total height of the plant.

Cultivars Recommended for Quarter Standard

Bon Accord	Lyes Unique
Chang	Margaret Roe
Cloverdale Pearl	Micky Goult
Countess of Aberdeen	Icecap
Dusky Beauty	Tom Thumb
Lindisfarne	White Joy

Half and Full Standards

Exactly the same method of growth will be used for the half standard and the full standard, although the measurements will vary. For a half standard it is necessary to have a clear stem of between 18 and 30 inches (46–76cm), and for a full standard the measurement is between 30 and 42 inches (76–107cm). These are the measurements accepted by the British Fuchsia Society in their show schedules and are the measurements used by most of the affiliated societies. The measurements are taken from the compost in the pot to the first break on the stem. That break can be either a branch or a leaf. The stem should be as straight as possible and may be supported by a stake. This stake should be in proportion to the size of the trunk and should be neatly tied to the trunk of the plant. The stem should be clean and as free of any scarring as possible.

**Cultivars Recommended
for Half and Full Standards**

Those recommended for use as quarter standards can be used for this type of growth.

Annabel	Lady Isobel Barnett
Barbara	Marin Glow
Celia Smedley	Marinka
Checkerboard	Mrs Lovell Swisher
Display	Royal Velvet
Dollar Princess	Rufus the Red
Flirtation Waltz	Snowcap
Foxtrot	Swingtime
Jack Shahan	Tennessee Waltz
Joy Patmore	Tom West

Small Pot Culture Standard

The table standard or the standard grown under the rules for small pot culture is a relative newcomer to the show bench but one that I think should be well contested as the plants so produced are very attractive. The rules for growing plants under small pot culture are quite simple – the pot should not exceed 5 inches (13cm) in diameter and the clear stem of the mini-standard should not exceed 10 inches (25cm) in length. There is no minimum length laid down but I would suggest, to get a good balanced plant, that a minimum of 7 inches (18cm) should be aimed at.

I like this class as it is possible to grow a mini-standard in one season very successfully from a cutting taken early in the year. It is possible, in fact advisable, to use cultivars which have small flowers as they will look more in proportion to the final size of the plant. If you would like to be really adventurous why not try using some of the members of the *Encliandra* group such as Lottie Hobby or *x. bacillaris*. They have extremely small flowers and small foliage, their stems are very willowy and to succeed in getting even a miniature standard from this type of plant is very satisfying and gives a great sense of achievement. For someone anxious to try the art of growing standards for the first time, then the small pot culture size is an excellent one to start on.

**Cultivars Recommended
for Small Pot Culture Standards**

Alison Ewart	Lottie Hobby
Eleanor Leytham	Micky Goult
General Monk	Nellie Nuttall
Lady Thumb	Son of Thumb
Liebriez	Tom Thumb
Lindisfarne	*x. bacillaris*

Baskets

An excellent way to exhibit your fuchsias is by growing them in baskets. When these are placed just above eye-level it is possible to appreciate the full beauty of the flowers by looking up into them. Baskets can be either the full, free hanging basket or what are sometimes described as half or wall baskets. These are half the size of a full basket and fit snugly against the wall.

It is possible to purchase many different shapes of baskets made from a variety of materials, but for the purpose of entering BFS shows the baskets must be of hemi-spherical shape (half a circle) and the wall baskets should be demi-hemi-spherical. There has been considerable discussion over the years as to whether flat-bottomed baskets should be eligible for competition but at the moment of writing such baskets are not permitted in BFS shows although they might be acceptable in local shows. It does not matter whether the baskets are made of wire or plastic – either is equally acceptable.

Plants for baskets should be either autumn or very early spring cuttings. There are many different cultivars from which you can choose although I feel that the most attractive basket of fuchsias should contain just one variety. Some people think that using a number of different cultivars makes a more attractive basket, but this is not usually so as differing cultivars develop and grow at different rates and an uneven basket would result.

Baskets vary in size – for a 10 inch (25cm) diameter basket I would suggest using four plants, three around the edge and one in the centre to give extra height. For a 15 inch (38cm) basket, six plants might be more appropriate, although a lot will depend upon the strength and vigour of the cultivar chosen.

The plants for a basket need to be quite well developed before planting out. An early spring cutting should be grown on steadily in a 3 inch (7½cm) pot and should be encouraged to get as bushy as possible by taking out the growing tip (pinching out) after three pairs of leaves have been formed. When each of the resulting shoots has grown three pairs of leaves the tips should be removed once again from all of the shoots. If you allow them to grow on, still in their 3 inch (7½cm) pots, then you will have excellent plants for using in your baskets.

The compost you need for basket work should be a good peat-based compost – a soil-based compost would become extremely heavy when watered. Place your basket in a bucket or a large flower pot, to keep it steady when you are filling it with compost. Two half baskets can be placed back to back and held in position whilst filling. The baskets should be lined, either with moss or with plastic. If you use plastic, make sure that some drainage holes are made before filling.

Half fill the basket with the compost and then place four empty 3 inch (7½cm) pots in position on the compost, one between each of the supporting wires and one in the centre. Fill the whole of the basket, including the pots, with the compost. When you remove the pots you will have left perfect indentations the exact size of the root ball on your plants. Remove the plants from their pots and place them in the indentations. Tap the basket on the bench and the plants will be in their correct positions.

It is possible to prepare the baskets at about the end of April with good sized plants, but do not contemplate putting them outside until the beginning of June at the earliest, as frosts are likely to be a possibility until about that time. Keep them in the greenhouse where they will grow rapidly and build up

Planting a Hanging Basket

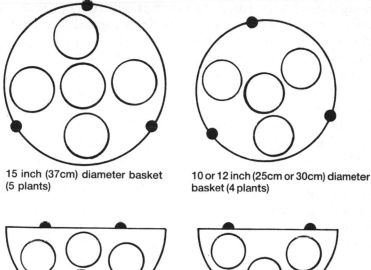

15 inch (37cm) diameter basket
(5 plants)

10 or 12 inch (25cm or 30cm) diameter
basket (4 plants)

15 inches (37cm) across rear of basket
(4 plants)

12 inches (30cm) across rear of basket
(3 plants)

into fine baskets of plants. Pinch out the growing tips of the shoots as soon as they develop three pairs of leaves, to encourage as many side growths as possible. This will be, towards the end of the preparation season, quite a mammoth task as there will be many hundreds of side shoots.

Once your baskets are ready to be placed outside, from the beginning of June, no further pinching out of the tips should be necessary unless you are growing your baskets for a specific show. If you are growing for your own pleasure then they should be allowed to flower as soon as they wish. Regular feeding and watering of the plants will be necessary during the season as baskets tend to dry out rather quickly. The positioning of the basket is not of great importance although some cultivars are more amenable to full sun than others. Keep an eye open for pests and diseases, and carry out a regular spraying programme.

Biennial Baskets

It is also possible to grow a basket which will be used from year to year – in fact a basket grown using the biennial method of cultivation will be similar to those which cause such great interest in national shows. The basic method of producing the basket is similar to that already described, the major difference being that it will not be allowed to flower during the first season.

Plants for this type of basket can be produced from cuttings rooted in late spring. At this time the plants will grow and develop rapidly. They should be allowed to grow in 3 inch (7½cm) and then 4 inch (10cm) pots, pinching out the growing tips at two pairs of leaves. In a very short space of time good bushy plants will have been formed. From the middle of June to the beginning of July, the plants can be put into their baskets. Five to a 14 or 15 inch (35cm or 38cm) basket would be ideal, although it is not unknown for the really expert growers to use just one plant in a basket of that size. The plants will be encouraged to grow rapidly and pinching out will continue. By feeding with a high nitrogren type feed luxurious growth will be achieved. Do not let the plants starve or they will be inclined to start forming flower buds, which should not be allowed during the first year.

At the start of autumn, perhaps in September or October, the basket may need a slight rest from its rapid growth. The watering and the feeding should be reduced so that it becomes semi-dormant. At the same time it is advisable to trim back the longer growths of the plants, so that there is a mound of good, strong, thick growth in the upper part of the basket, forming a semicircle. The basket will form the lower part of the complete circle. Remove the whole of the plant section from the basket and give the whole lot a good clean. Whilst it is separate from the basket it is easier to remove all the dead leaves and debris that there may be.

The plants will not be allowed to rest completely and in the spring it will be an easy task to revitalise them. Again remove from the basket, clean out the top, and slice off the bottom half to two thirds of the root system, which will be a close mat of roots. Place a quantity of fresh compost in the basket, replace the plants, and then sprinkle fresh compost on top of the root ball so that the basket is completely full. No space will be needed at the top as the process of watering will cause the compost to settle leaving sufficient space for future watering.

The basket should be given preferential treatment for a few days, keeping it shaded from any hot sun, spraying overhead two or three times a day and encouraging it to send out fresh shoots. As shoots develop they should be stopped at every two pairs of leaves and the growths should be encouraged to cascade down over the edge of the basket, so that eventually, the basket will be completely hidden. Continue to feed regularly and watch the basket grow.

At every opportunity the basket should be placed outside the greenhouse in the fresh air. After the end of May, or when all risk of frosts has passed, the basket should be placed permanently outside on its own basket stand. This is necessary at this stage as you might already have had difficulty in transporting a wide basket through the doors of the greenhouse. Ensure that the plants remain free from any pests and diseases and keep pinching out the growths – but remember to stop in good time so that flower buds will have ample opportunity to develop before the show.

Your major problem now is to find some way of transporting a superb basket to shows, but this I am sure is something which you will enjoy solving. It may have taken two years to grow but you will have a superb basket and one that, with the same type of treatment, can continue for a number of years. The vital point is that top growth can only grow when there is equal movement and growth of the roots below.

I have recommended planting only fuchsias in your basket. I think this is the most attractive way to display your fuchsias although I must admit I have seen some beautiful baskets made up with a variety of different types of flowers and incorporating just one or two fuchsias. There are many different types of plants that you can use and I am sure that a fuchsia will complement any of them.

Half Baskets

Half baskets are planted in a similar way to the full baskets, but for a 10 inch (25cm) half basket three plants are placed around the front edge and one plant in the centre at the back to fill in the basket. For half baskets I favour the smaller flowered cultivars but that is a matter of personal preference.

As with full baskets it is possible to grow your half baskets using the biennial method. By this means it is possible to grow very large half or wall baskets with long hanging branches fully clothed with flowers. One of the major problems with half baskets, and an area where a great many exhibitors fall down, is in the failure to completely clothe the plants with bloom. Far too often these structures are seen with blooms on the ends of the laterals but only bare foliage in the basket area. It is important therefore to build up a good dome of young foliage in the upper part of the basket so that flowers are plentiful when required.

The transportation of half baskets is also a problem although with a large vehicle it is possible to lay the whole plant down on a flat surface – the snag is that there is very little room left for other plants being transported at the same time.

Cultivars Recommended for Full and Half Baskets

Annabel	Lena
Auntie Jinks	Marinka
Autumnale	Pink Galore
Blush of Dawn	Pink Marshmallow
Cascade	President Margaret Slater
Charlie Gardiner	President Stanley Wilson
Daisy Bell	Princessita
Frosted Flame	Rose of Denmark
Golden Marinka	Sophisticated Lady
Harry Gray	Stanley Cash
Jack Acland	Swingtime
Jack Shanan	Vanessa Jackson
La Campanella	

Hanging Pots

Another comparatively recent introduction to fuchsia growing is the hanging pot. These are usually pots of 6 or 8 inch (15–20cm) diameter. In some shows such pots are used to show just one plant but in others it is possible to grow more than one. Again, I would suggest if more than one plant is being used then they should be all of the same cultivar. For decorative purposes, three plants of a small flowering cultivar in a 6 inch (15cm) or 8 inch (18cm) pot are ideal. There are many cultivars from which you can choose. The advent of these hanging pots does mean that you can display plants from smaller brackets from the sides of houses or bungalows without the risk of them being bashed against the wall in high winds. They are also easier to take down and examine for pests and diseases during the course of the season. Again though, do not attempt to put such pots into position permanently until all risk of frosts has passed.

Cultivars Recommended for Hanging Pots

Daisy Bell	Postiljon
Derby Imp	Princessita
Harry Gray	Westminster Chimes
La Campanella	

(Try any small flowered cultivars with rather lax growth habit)

Small Pot Culture

It is also possible to grow plants of any shape in miniature. Quite simply, the plant must be in a pot not exceeding 5 inches (13cm) in diameter, with an overall height from soil level of not more than 20 inches (51cm). I am sure it is possible to have quite a lot of fun growing this shape of plant although it is fair to say that shapes, other than miniature standards, are rarely seen on the show benches. But when they do appear they are undoubtedly a source of great admiration. I think it is a pity that more are not seen as it might encourage many more people to experiment.

Mini-fan

Often, a plant will refuse to make a round symmetrical shape but seems to want to grow rather flat. Why not make use of this – train it into the shape of a fan. By inserting a framework of flower canes (I find that the 30 inch (76cm) ones have the greatest strength for this purpose) you can gently persuade the branches to grow in the direction you desire. By carefully tying in the side shoots, and removing those which are out of position, it is possible quite quickly, in fact in one season, to build up a very attractive shape.

Having grown it as a small pot culture plant during the first year, progress from that in subsequent years by potting on into larger pots, adding further, stronger framework and training your plant into one of those super specimens so rarely seen. The whole process will take a number of years with your plant getting a little larger each year but again the satisfaction will be immense.

Mini-pillar

A pillar is a relatively easy shape to grow and can be considered as a combination of bush growth and standard growth on the same plant. A good strong cutting should be chosen of a cultivar which is self branching. When the cutting has formed two or three pairs of leaves the growing tip should be pinched out. This will result in shoots coming from the leaf axils and two shoots from the place where the tip was removed. Both of these shoots should be allowed to grow but all others should be rubbed out. These two shoots should now be treated as separate plants and should be separately tied to a cane that has been inserted beside the plant.

Decide on an ultimate height you wish your plant to achieve, and then allow one of the shoots to grow to half of that height before removing the growing tip. This will of course stimulate the growth of side shoots from that stem and they should be encouraged to grow round and cover the other stem. The second stem will be allowed to continue growing upwards until the final height is achieved and this too should then be stopped. All the side shoots that now form from each of these stems should be stopped at every two pairs of leaves to encourage bushy but even growth. The object really is to get a straight pillar of foliage and flowers.

Mini-pyramid

A pyramid is a much more difficult shape to achieve successfully. A vigorous free branching cultivar is required. A good strong growing cutting should be chosen early in spring and allowed to grow up to about 6 inches (15cm) in height. All the side shoots should be allowed to develop. When the plant has reached that height then the growing tip should be removed. From the resulting two shoots select one and allow it to grow on, but remove the other one. The growing shoot should be supported by a cane and allowed to grow on for another 6 inches (15cm) when the operation should be repeated – the growing tip removed and the two resulting shoots allowed to grow. One of the shoots should be rubbed out again, but this time ensure it is the one from the opposite side to the first one removed so that the stem can continue to grow evenly in an upward direction. Throughout this process of getting height attention needs to be paid to the laterals from the stem, to keep the shape as like a pyramid as possible, i.e. it needs to be much broader at the base and tapering to the top. Symmetry is what you must be aiming for, but it will need a great deal of luck. It is important with this type of training to ensure that the growth is not retarded in any way so a system of potting on and feeding is necessary to encourage this continuous growth. The size of the final pot for a mini-pyramid should be 5 inches (13cm) but if you are not confining yourself to a maximum height of 20 inches (51cm) then the upward growth will be determined by the size of the pots being used.

These are only a few of the formal shapes that can be used for your plants. Do not feel that you have to confine yourself to these – be adventurous and experiment. Why not grow a 'crown of fuchsias' or a ring or a hoop, or any other shape that takes your fancy. Try multi-plant structures and, to make these even more interesting, why not try multi-variety structures. In an American publication I have seen a type of standard fuchsia which had been trained rather like a poodle-clipped plant. The ideas must be legion but have fun with your plants and show what can be done.

(Recommended cultivars for these methods of training are included in the section on large structures. It is not advisable to grow very large structures using the methods described above, so any of the strong growing cultivars which you particularly like will be suitable.)

FEEDING

To get really good plants of any type, it is necessary to feed them. The compost in which the plants are growing contains a certain amount of nutrients but not sufficient to maintain good active growth throughout the season. If additional food is not given the plants will cease to grow, will look starved and, because they feel threatened will try to produce their flowers prematurely.

In the same way that we require a good balanced diet to keep us healthy, so do the plants. The food given to plants to keep them healthy consists of nitrogen, phosphates and potash together with many trace elements. We are fortunate these days in that we can obtain well-balanced feeds for our plants – in any garden centre you will see bottles and packets of plant foods. All are useful but it is wise to examine the labels of the containers carefully so that the right food is given at the right time.

Examine any bottle or packet and you will see the letters N, P and K being used to indicate the percentage of each element that is available in the food. Nitrogen (N) stimulates the growth of leaves, giving a healthy look to the foliage and building up the plant. It is obvious therefore that a compost high in nitrogen will be required in the early part of the season, when we are anxious to have strong growth to build up a large plant.

Phosphates (P) help to build up a good strong root system so are essential again at the beginning of the season when we require that quick growth. Potash (K) is absolutely essential in that it assists the plant to make use of the nitrogen content of the feed, helps to prevent soft, sappy growth and helps to improve the colour of the flowers. It is very useful towards the end of the season therefore in ripening the plants and encouraging them to flower.

I like to buy fertilizer in powder or granular form, so that I can add my own water. The feeds I use regularly are the Chempak Liquid Feed Fertilizers, which come in handy packets which are capable of making up to four hundred gallons of full strength liquid feed, and are thus quite economical. Chempak make eight different types of liquid fertilizer, numbered from 1 to 8. The three formulations which interest us most are the No.2, No.3, and No.4.

If you examine the packet of Formula 2 you will notice the description 'high nitrogen 25–15–15'. (The first number always refers to nitrogen, the second to the phosphates and the third to the potash.) This, as the packet states, gives an early season boost for all plants. Formula 3 is one that I would suggest you use during the main growing season. It is a balanced 20–20–20 and is described as an all year round feed. Chempak No. 4 has a high potash formula, 15–15–30. This is therefore very useful at the end of the season when we require the maturing and subsequent flowering of the plants. All of these feeds also contain seven additional trace elements which are vital for the well-being of plants. They are magnesium, iron, manganese, copper, zinc, boron and molybdenum.

Nothing is gained by exceeding the quantity of crystals that you use when feeding your plants, so it is important to follow the instructions on the side of the packet. The recommended strength of feed for each of these fertilizers is one level teaspoon of crystals in one gallon of water fed weekly during the growing season. They also suggest that a more frequent feeding at quarter strength will be beneficial, perhaps each time you water plants – that is, one level teaspoonful with four gallons of water. I must admit that I always prefer to use the diluted feed – at least this way I do not have to remember when last I fed my plants.

It is also possible to purchase another feed called Vitafeed Liquid Fertilizer. The two types normally recommended for fuchsias are the 3–0–1 and 1–0–3 Vitafeeds. These feeds do without the phosphates and concentrate strongly on a very high nitrogen content or a very high potash content. They also contain trace elements but I am a little anxious about the lack of phosphates when one considers how important they are in the development of the roots. However, I do use these fertilizers as an additional boost to my plants when I wish them to make quicker growth, and would recommend them.

There is another very well-known powder form of feed often recommended for use when growing fuchsias, Phostrogen. This is an excellent feed but if you examine the formula you will notice that it is very high in potash. This does mean that plants fed with Phostrogen throughout the season tend to become mature and therefore rather hard in the wood, fairly early in the season. I would certainly recommend using this product from the middle to the end of the season as it does give plants a greater depth of colour. It is also extremely useful for feeding plants in troughs or in the open garden.

One of the trace elements which is vital to the healthy growth of any plant is magnesium. Occasionally the supply of magnesium in a compost becomes exhausted, the shortage becoming obvious when the leaves develop yellow streaks and spots. The lower leaves of a plant will often drop leaving a rather bare looking stem. If this is caused by a magnesium deficiency, which is one of the possible reasons, it can be remedied by giving the plant a dose of Epsom salts. A level tablespoonful of Epsom salts in a gallon of water applied on two or three occasions as soon as the deficiency is noticed will rectify the situation. Epsom salts can be bought in fairly large quantities at most garden centres, under the name of magnesium sulphate, at a reasonable price.

Fuchsias will also benefit from feeding through the leaves, that is foliar feeding. The Chempak fertilizers can be used for this purpose and, as the crystals are very soluble in water they do not leave unsightly stains on the leaves. Other powder feeds do tend to have this fault. This of course will not matter if you are growing your plants just for fun but if you are growing seriously with the show bench in mind, white powder marks on the foliage would be a disadvantage. There are some brands made especially for this purpose – Double F (Foliar Feed) instantly comes to mind. Plants which have suffered a traumatic experience at root level will certainly benefit from a foliar feed boost.

Plants which are growing out in the garden should also be fed, although, having prepared the ground well before planting, there will be a good reservoir of food available. However, it is beneficial during the growing season to give the plants a feed regularly with any of the feeds I have mentioned.

To sum up I would say that fuchsias are gross feeders and will amply repay an effort made to ensure that they have a good balanced diet throughout the season. A good strong healthy growing plant is less likely to succumb to any diseases that might be present in the area. Little and often is perhaps the best way to describe my method of feeding – too much, infrequently, causes the plant the equivalent of indigestion. They will only take up what they need from the compost so excessive amounts will simply cause the compost to go stale and will, in any case, be wasted.

One final word of warning. Feeding should never be carried out when the compost is dry – always ensure that the plants are in a good moist compost. Failure to do so might increase the danger of the roots being damaged by the chemicals contained in the food.

OVER-WINTERING

One of the questions asked, perhaps more often than any other, is 'How do we look after our fuchsias during the winter?' The difficulty is that there is no one answer that can be given. Each grower's problems are different to any other's, and the solutions will depend on the number and type of plants you have, and the conditions in which they are growing.

If you have no greenhouse, growing plants mainly out in the garden with a few in tubs growing as bushes and as standards, the plants will have been removed from their pots and planted fairly deeply in early June. If this advice has been followed, I would suggest that the plants should be left where they are in the garden to fend for themselves. Many of the plants you have outside may not be considered to be the hardy varieties, and, whilst it is technically unsafe to leave them out, if we give them the opportunity of showing us how sturdy they are we might well be very surprised.

As autumn approaches I would suggest giving them a little extra protection around the base by giving them a good mulch with peat, or grass clippings, well-weathered ashes, or bracken or, in fact, anything which will give them some insulation against severe and deep frosts. Our object is to protect the root system from becoming frozen as it is from here that new growth will come in the spring. If plants were planted out in early June then they have had the chance to build up a good root system. If the planting out was delayed until July or later it is possible that such a good rooting system will not have been formed. In this case it might be advisable to lift the plants when frosts are threatened and take them into a frost free place.

Plants which are to be left outside can be left to continue flowering until the first severe frosts arrive and cause all the leaves to fall. Being scrupulously clean in our gardens the temptation will naturally be there to remove all the dead-looking branches from the bushes. Please don't – tidy up the plants a little if you like, but leave them in position, for two reasons. Firstly they will of course mark the positions of the plants for next year and secondly they will provide a certain amount of protection from the frosts.

If you wish, as autumn progresses, you might take out a simple insurance policy so that you do not lose the variety in the garden. Simply take a cutting from each plant, root them in a minimum of warmth, and keep them growing steadily through the winter. They will require a minimum of attention and will ensure that you have a young plant of each of the varieties you have outside, in the spring. (The method of taking and looking after these cuttings is described in the section 'Taking Cuttings', *see* page 58.)

If your plants are in tubs and pots but you have no green-house protection, you must find somewhere where they can be kept frost free during the winter. Such a position could be a spare room, a shed, a garage or even a cold frame. The object is to keep the root system free of frosts, but it must also be prevented from drying out completely. A large box, in a garage or shed, lined with paper or polystyrene tiles would be ideal for keeping the root system moist.

Leave the wintering of these plants as long as you possibly can. Keep an eye on the weather forecasts and if frosts are threatened take your plants, in their pots, under cover. When it is absolutely essential to take the plants in permanently, I suggest giving them a very thorough cleaning. If you remove the plants from their pots you will find it easier to remove any debris that may have accumulated on the surface of the compost. Prune back the top growth so that you are left with about two-thirds of each branch. This will ease the problems of storage slightly. Remove all the foliage from the plant – completely defoliate it. Naturally it is better to carry out this task out of doors. Having defoliated the plant you will have removed any diseased or infected leaves that may have been present.

When you have completed this task with all the plants you wish to store, give them all a very thorough spraying with a combined insecticide and fungicide. At least then you will be sure that you are not storing trouble for the winter. The compost of these plants needs to be just moist – not too wet and not too dry. It is fatal to allow them to become too dry – more plants are lost through over-dryness than through excessive wetness. The plants can be placed in this large box or container, covered with an insulating material (dry peat or layers of newspaper would be ideal) and left undisturbed in the frost free environment. An occasional examination during the winter months to ensure that they have not dried out is advisable.

This advice applies to all types of fuchsia growth, shrubs, bushes, or standards. If you have standards growing in the garden, out of their pots, do not leave them there as I have advised for bush plants as the very first severe frost will kill the stem of the standard and the plant will have been lost. Standards must be taken inside and given the same treatment as recommended for bushes except that the branches should be reduced by about a half. Once they have been defoliated they can be left lying in the box, one on top of each other, before covering them with insulating material. Plants growing in baskets can be either left in their baskets or removed and dealt with separately.

Young plants which were taken as cuttings later in the season should be kept in a light airy, frost free position, so that they can continue to grow steadily through the winter. They will retain their leaves but little additional growth will be made until lighter and warmer conditions prevail. They should be kept in a minimum temperature of 40 degrees Fahrenheit (5°C) but should not be much warmer or thin spindly growth will result.

If you have a greenhouse then the suggestions already made will apply to you unless you are prepared to offer the plants an environment with a reasonable growing temperature of 45 degrees (7°C) plus. As the plants are deciduous I think it is better to allow them to have a rest during the winter months. Plants should therefore be prepared in the same way as previously recommended, making sure that any diseases are removed from the plants before returning them to a spotlessly clean greenhouse. If it is possible, a part of the greenhouse could be partitioned off so that a slightly higher temperature can be maintained. If this is done then a temperature of 40 degrees Fahrenheit (5°C) for the plants standing on the staging of the greenhouse would be ideal. I am not really in favour of placing the plants under the staging as this is undoubtedly the coldest part of the house. Nevertheless this is a method carried out by many leading growers where space is at a premium. Again I would suggest that you keep an eye on the weather forecast and if frost is forecast then additional protection with sheets of newspaper will be beneficial.

Many people, with completely unheated greenhouses, bury their plants in the border of their houses covering the plants with straw and paper before completing the covering with a layer of soil. Another method used by some people without any protection whatsoever is to bury plants in a trench in the garden which has been lined with straw, covering the plants with straw before filling in the trench with soil and marking the site for future reference. This is an extremely successful method although I must admit it is rather hard work. The plants come through very successfully and when removed from their 'graves', when all fear of frosts is passed, they usually have long white growths showing that they are still alive. These growths should be cut back and soon take on a fresh green look.

To sum up, if plants are to survive the winter, they need to be kept frost free, the root ball needs to be kept slightly moist, and the foliage with all its attendant diseases needs to be removed. With a modicum of luck you should be able to get your complete collection through the winter ready to give you another excellent display the following season.

4
Hybridisation

It is a natural desire to improve. In the athletics world there is the desire to run faster, jump higher or further, throw a greater distance; in fact whereever you look, in whatever field of life, there is the anxiety to achieve perfection. But perfection is an elusive quality and when one goal has been achieved another appears before you. So it is in the plant world – hybridists are forever striving to produce plants which are more colourful, vegetables which are more prolific, strains which are resistant to diseases

Bringing the microscope of life in much closer to concentrate on a very small part of botany, the fuchsia, how have our hybridisers progressed over the years? Are they keeping up with our modern demands? Do they have the knowledge at their disposal to produce plants to a set pattern of the shape, size and colour they desire? With the advancement of knowledge in modern genetics it is possible that one day such objectives will be achieved; but not yet. It is still a mystery when one plant is crossed with another as to what the resulting progeny will be like. And this I suppose is the fascination of the hybridists art – not knowing, and waiting for the first flowers from a new batch of seedlings to appear, gives that wonderful feeling of excitement.

But what are our hybridists trying to achieve? Do we not have sufficient different cultivars already at our disposal? Is their search for the different improving or weakening the strain? The answer to the first question is a desire to improve by producing flowers with different colourings, different shapes and forms, foliage which is stronger and more colourful, and plants which are more disease resistant and strong enough to withstand low temperatures. To be successful our hybridisers need to be ruthless in their approach and scientific in their methods.

The fuchsia has only been known for just over two centuries. In that span of time it is possible that weaknesses have been bred into many of our plants, but it is also possible that the desired characteristics of colour and strength have been achieved. It is also possible, if a particular experiment has failed, to return to our sources, the species, and start again. This approach has been carried out by some of our scientific hybridists with interesting and fascinating results. We should build on these successes and progress from them. Only by a ruthless culling of those plants in a new batch of seedlings which do not carry the desired traits will we be able to strengthen our stocks and not weaken them.

It is fair to say therefore that unless you have the instinct to throw away those plants which are unsuitable, you should not progress into the realms of the hybridists. Having said that, it must be added that it is the ambition of most keen growers of any type of plant to produce something which is different from any produced before. Long may this ambition continue as it is generally left to the amateur grower and hybridist to produce the exciting new colours which prove so popular.

Bearing in mind that the number of cultivars has reached the eight thousand mark, and is still climbing, it seems an almost impossible task to find something absolutely new. Far too often I am afraid when 'new' cultivars are brought on to the market they are found to be very similar to something already in existence and no improvement upon it. What we are looking for are plants which are going to make excellent bushy growth with a minimum of training from us. They therefore need to be short jointed and self branching. They need to be capable of producing many flowers, continuously, over a long season. They should be strong and resistant to the vagaries of the weather, and capable of overcoming the onslaughts of pests and diseases. The flowers need to be of good shape and form and of interesting colour combinations. They need to be produced at a very early stage in the development of the plant and should present themselves boldly for all to admire. They should also be capable of producing viable seeds and pollen so that further advances can be made as and when needed.

These objectives are not beyond reach, but it is necessary to work steadily towards any goal and not to become satisfied with inferior products or too disappointed with apparent lack of success. Hybridising is not a hit-or-miss occupation, it is something which requires careful control and tabulation. Records of all crosses should be carefully kept and made, I hope, available to others so that they can continue with a line which may have been abandoned.

Flower Structure

Before considering in detail the act of cross pollination it is important to have an understanding of the various parts which make up the structure of the fuchsia flower. Starting at the point where the flower is attached to the stem of the plant we find the *pedicel* or stalk. This can vary quite considerably in length. There are a number of cultivars whose beauty is enhanced by the way in which the flower hangs down and away from the stem on a long pedicel. The pedicel leads down to the *ovary,* which consists of four separate compartments, containing the ovules. These, when fertilised, become the seeds. Although on first examination of an unfertilised ovary there appear to be a vast number of these ovules, there will not be a corresponding large number of seeds after fertilisation – in fact it is often found that fully ripened seed pods contain very few viable seeds.

The *tube* or hypanthium is a protective covering for the long stamens and pistil. The colour of the tube varies considerably from plant to plant and is a very attractive part of the complete flower. Some hybridists aim to produce flowers with a specific colouring of the tube and this, over the years, has become their hall mark. On most fuchsia flowers there are four sepals located at the end of the tube. In fact it is considered that any plants showing flowers bearing more than four sepals are not true to form. It has become quite common in recent years to find many plants of well-known cultivars which carry flowers bearing five or even more sepals – this is rather arbitrarily considered a fault. Perhaps the time will come when such flowers are accepted as attractive and welcomed in the same way as the first plants that were developed bearing in excess of the four petals found on the species. Botanically speaking, the sepals of any flower are really modified leaves whose main purpose in life is to protect the stigma, anthers and petals prior to their development into their full-flowering glory. However, the colouring of the sepals of the fuchsia has become an important consideration and it is the comparison of the colouring of the sepals and petals which gives the flower so much of its appeal.

Grouped beneath the sepals are a number of petals, collectively known as the *corolla*. With a flower that is classified as a single there are just four petals; a semi-double flower has five, six or seven petals, and a full double has eight or more. Without doubt the more petals there are, the fuller the flower

The Fuchsia Flower

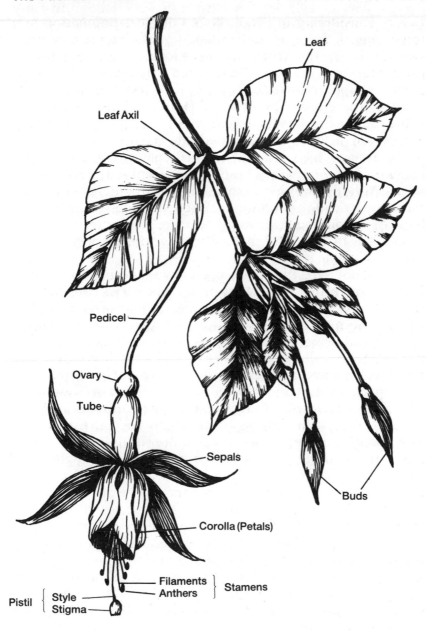

Leaf

Leaf Axil

Pedicel

Ovary

Tube

Sepals

Buds

Corolla (Petals)

Filaments }
Anthers } Stamens

Pistil { Style
Stigma

Single Flower = 4 petals
Semi-double Flower = 5, 6 or 7 petals
Double Flower = 8+ petals

appears and the more attractive it becomes. The colouring of the corolla is a vital part of the attraction – it can be almost any colour from the most delicate pastel shades to the richest and deepest hues. There are reds, blues, oranges, whites, purples and almost any combination of these colours. Up to the present time no true yellow colour has been achieved, although some modern hybridists feel that they are getting close to this elusive goal. One of the most famous of recent hybridists, the late Cliff Gadsby, did in fact produce a flower which was primrose yellow in colour. Many growers would probably have been satisfied with this success, but such was the dedication of Cliff Gadsby that, as it was not considered to be of sufficient depth of colour and intensity, it was consigned to the compost heap. I hope that hybridists of the future will have the same sense of dedication.

The corolla surrounds the sexual organs of the flower and of course plays its part in attracting the carrier of the pollen. The sexual parts of the flower are the *stamens* and the *pistil*. There are usually eight stamens, consisting of thin filaments at the end of which are found the *anthers*. The anthers are like small pads from which the pollen is obtained. Protruding through the stamens is a longer stalk known as the *style*, at the end of which is another pad called a *stigma*. This stigma, when it is in the correct condition to be fertilised, becomes rather sticky. It is then ready to receive grains of pollen from either its own stamens or from other plants nearby, carried either on the wind or by insects. In the natural habitat of the fuchsia, the pollinating process is carried out by humming birds, whose long beaks have become specially adapted to the long tubes of the flowers.

Cross-fertilisation

The act of hybridisation should not be undertaken lightly but some considerable thought should be given to the objectives and the plants that you are likely to use. It might be a good thing to make a conscious effort towards the end of one season to decide what your breeding programme is going to be the following year. Plants that you are going to use can then be brought back into growth following their winter rest, very early in the season. The plants should be treated as normal, repotting them and placing them in fresh compost, carrying out the normal pruning session and then allowing them to grow on undisturbed. Potting on can take place but only up into the 5 inch pot size. With second year plants this will mean that the pots will rapidly become filled with roots and the plants will, because of the lack of root growth, feel threatened and start to produce their flowers at a very early stage. The earlier in the season these crosses can take place, the larger the resultant seedlings will be before the onset of the winter.

The pollen-bearing flowers need a longer period of time to mature than the seed-bearing flowers so it is advisable to allow the first flush of flowers to remain on the plant, developing the pollen side of the operation. When it is obvious that the pollen is ripe, and this can be seen by the grains of pollen falling on to the petals, then the process of cross-pollination can start. Make sure now that you have all the equipment that you require ready. You will need a pair of scissors with fine points, some small muslin bags with which the fertilised flower will be covered (or some other such material for covering) and labels with which the fertilised flowers can be marked with the date of the cross and the pollinator.

Choose now, as the female flower, a bud that is just in the process of opening. Continue the process by 'popping' the bud (a slight pressure at the tip of the flower bud is usually sufficient). With the fine-pointed scissors, the process of emasculating the flower should now take place. This is simply a matter of cutting away all the petals and the stamens so that only the stigma is left. These stamens are removed so that there is no possibility of the flower self-pollinating after the completion of the operation. Hopefully, the stigma will feel slightly sticky or tacky to the touch. With a stamen from the male flower, gently brush the tip of the stigma so that pollen adheres to it. On completion of this operation affix a label showing the cross used, giving the name of the female flower first, followed by the pollen bearer (for example Joy Patmore × Marin Glow). The operation will be completed once the muslin bag, or protective covering, encloses the fertilised flower.

The operation should now be repeated, but this time the cross should be carried out in reverse. The plant used for the pollen should now be used as the seed parent and the original seed parent should provide the pollen. Again a record should be kept by affixing a label to the flower (for example Marin Glow × Joy Patmore). As with all things in gardening it is useful to include the date on which the cross is made. A record of these crosses should be kept in a diary retained especially for this purpose, so that the results can later be entered. Do not leave the recording of these details to your memory – the memory is a particularly fickle thing and it would be a shame if the parentage of an unusual new cultivar was not known for certain.

The miracle of reproduction must now be left to nature. The pollen grains adhering to the stigma will, if conditions are favourable, start to germinate and send microscopic tubes down the style into the *ovary* and then into the *ovum*. When this tube is complete the male gamete will be able to pass through the tube and join the female, forming a fertilised seed. The number of seeds that develop in the ovary will depend largely upon the strength of the pollen and its germination following the pollination. Conditions are most favourable for this operation and subsequent growth of the pollen tubes if the temperature is in the range of 70–75 degrees Fahrenheit (21–24°C).

It is now a question of patience and waiting for the ripening of the seed pods. About eight weeks will elapse before they are completely ready, by which time they will have taken on a very dark purple, almost black, look. If ripe they will, when gently lifted, fall away from the parent plant. By now it could easily be the beginning of August, and the decision has to be made whether you have the right sort of conditions to grow your young seedlings throughout the winter or whether the seeds should be stored for sowing early in the following year. Many growers are of the opinion that the greatest success is obtained if the seed is sown whilst it is absolutely fresh, as fuchsia seeds tend to lose their viability rather quickly under storage. However, if your conditions are such that it would be unwise to sow directly, then keep the seed pods intact during the winter rather than separate the seeds, and store them in that way. Whichever method you use please remember to keep the seed or the seed pod with its correct label.

To remove the seed from the ripe pod, crush the pod between the fingers and then wash them clean in a saucer of water, making sure that every piece of the covering of the seed pod is broken up and all the seed is washed out. The good seed will fall to the bottom of the saucer whilst the useless hulks will remain on the surface. Another method is to slice open the seed pod using a razor-blade and then remove the seeds from the pod with a pointed stick. A magnifying glass is a very useful instrument to have at this time so that the seed is more readily seen. With either method it is necessary to dry

Border Queen

Swingtime

Winston Churchill

Herald

Thalia

Tennessee Waltz

Dark Eyes

Jamboree

Blush of Dawn

Bealings

La Campanella

Marinka

Cloverdale Pearl

Lady I. Barnett

Display

Snowcap

the seed – placing them on some blotting paper and allowing them to dry naturally is perhaps the best method.

Growing the Seed

If you decide to sow immediately you will need to have a quantity of your usual compost available and some half pots into which they can be sown. Gently level the compost, not firming too harshly, and sprinkle the seed on to the surface. Again, gently press the seeds into the compost. Cover the pots with glass to prevent drying out of the compost and leave in a propagator with a temperature of around 60 degrees Fahrenheit (16°C). I do not recommend that you cover the seeds with any compost as it is considered by many growers that, in order to germinate to their greatest potential, fuchsia seeds require light. So, pressing the seeds into the compost will suffice. Watering may be carried out either by immersing the half pot in a tray of water so that the moisture is brought up from beneath, or by spraying overhead with a very fine spray.

Germination of fuchsia seed can be very erratic so again patience is a necessity. The process can vary from eighteen days to four months so do not be tempted to throw away any seed pans until all hope of germination has gone. The seedlings should be pricked out as soon as they can be handled, into individual compartments. I am in favour of using the multipot trays that are available especially the polystyrene trays which retain heat and allow you to remove the seedlings by pushing up from below.

When these young seedlings have grown sufficiently and have filled their pots with roots they should be potted on into 3 inch (7½cm) pots, each with its own label showing the cross, and grown on as strongly as possible. These plants could be potted on further into 4 inch (10cm) pots and allowed to flower there or, as some growers do, planted out in the garden during their first season. Plants grown outside are usually much sturdier and will provide good plants and copious cutting material if the flowers and plants are of sufficient quality. (Don't forget the labelling though.) With luck, plants from seeds sown in early autumn or at the beginning of the new year will be in flower during August so it will be possible to assess their suitability for future use.

When your new young seedlings come into flower it is advisable to get the assistance of another fuchsia enthusiast to help you evaluate your plants. It is possible that out of a batch of a hundred or more there will be one or two which immediately strike you as being different, showing the characteristics that you are looking for. It is more likely, however, that there will be none that instantly attract you but a fair number which, when seen together, and if their attributes were combined together, would go some way to achieving your goal. It is these young seedlings which could be of use to you in future years when proceeding with your programme of hybridisation – the process of retaining the strengths and disposing of the weaknesses. Two young seedlings each bearing some of the characteristics, such as colour of flower or vigour of growth, that you wish to fix could be used when making your next 'crosses'. Eventually, with luck and patience it might be possible to reach your objective.

To sum up, with a programme of hybridisation do not trust to luck but have a definite object in view. If you are anxious to produce a pure white, or a terminal flowering basket variety, or a pure yellow, then look for some of those characteristics in your choice of parents and gradually work towards your goal. Disappointment might well be the result for a number of years, but you never know, the next batch might bring success. Take the responsibility of producing new cultivars seriously, be meticulous in your recording of the parentage. Build up family trees in your record book, recording the failures as well as the successes. Share your knowledge so that others may benefit from your failures and successes – it is only by co-operation between like-minded people that eventual success can be achieved.

I have mentioned time and time again the necessity of keeping records. At the risk of offending many people I wonder about those seedsmen who produce fuchsia seed for sale in packets without any indication at all of the parentage of these seeds. There is bound to be the temptation to purchase such packets and to sow them. It is possible that some success will be achieved and that the seeds, or some of them, will germinate. The growers of these seedlings may not have the strength of character to decide that the cultivars they have raised are no good, no improvement upon fuchsias already in cultivation, and must therefore be thrown on the compost heap. It is a pity that such plants, the pride and joy of the growers, are passed on as cuttings to admiring friends. It is to be hoped of course that such plants will not pass the test of time and that their vigour will be such that within a couple of years they will be no more. However, it is not beyond the bounds of possibility that such packets may produce some new and exciting seedling. It has not been unknown for a seedling found growing accidentally in the gravel on a greenhouse bench to turn out to be a winner and to appear for many years on the show benches around the country. But such chance seedlings are the exception.

If you achieve success, do not rush to place your new cultivar on the market but wait for three or four years testing it out in as many ways as you can. Try growing it in different ways, training it to different shapes. Test it for its hardiness and its ability not only to withstand the winter weather but also to provide new shoots early in the season and flowers at an early date. Ask other enthusiastic growers to examine your plants and to comment upon them. After three or four years, if you are still happy with the plant, and are satisfied that it has retained its earlier glory, take it to a nurseryman so that it can be offered to the general public. Registration of the plant with the International Registration Body in America is the final act so that your 'baby' shall have a name not being used by any other. Grow your new plants as well as you can and compare them with other plants of the same type by exhibiting them in fuchsia shows – it is then, if success is yours, that you can sit back and bathe in the reflected glory of your new cultivar.

SPORTS

There are two methods by which new varieties of fuchsias become available to the grower. The first, which has been mentioned in detail elsewhere, is by crossing two different fuchsias and producing seed which, when germinated, produces a new plant. The second consists of a change within the structure of the plant as a result of which a new colour appears in the foliage or in the flower. This is called *sporting*. Over the years many new varieties have been discovered by this method. Usually it is quite a simple change, one branch of a plant appearing not with the normal green foliage but with a golden or variegated type of leaf. Occasionally a change occurs in the colour of the flower – generally this colour change is from a darker coloured corolla to a lighter coloured one. There have, however, been changes when the corolla has darkened in colour.

These sports, or mutations, are very interesting and they

have, over the years, produced a great number of worthwhile new cultivars. If it should be your good fortune to find a sport on a plant, it is important to secure and grow it for a number of years before sharing your new 'baby' with others, as there is always the risk that it will revert to its former colouring. It is also very interesting to note that quite often a plant, which has appeared quite stable over a number of years, starts to produce these mutations in one season in different parts of the country – from plants which apparently have no real connection. A problem arises, however, under these circumstances as each finder is anxious to record the new cultivar by giving it a name. This was the case with Border Queen which, in the same season in various parts of the country, produced branches with a golden foliage which were given various names.

Usually the sport appears on a single branch, which must be carefully noted. Cuttings should be taken from that branch – as many as possible, so it will be necessary to use the smallest of tips, or the minutest of buds in leaf axils. Grow them on carefully, ensuring that they are well-labelled and that the name of the plant from which they have been taken is known. If the change is in the colour of the leaf you may well need to take great care in the rooting process as it is often difficult to root cuttings with golden or variegated leaves.

The plants obtained from these cuttings should be grown on and flowered as soon as possible in order to see whether or not the change in the colour of the flower has been fixed. It is of course possible to see whether the changed leaf colour has been retained as the plant progresses through its stages.

Obviously for the changed colour of the flower to have been noticed it must have been sufficiently distinctive – the change from the parent to the offspring being a sufficient improvement to warrant keeping it and recording it as a new cultivar. As with new seedlings there is the awful temptation, as it is new and something that is peculiar to you, to think of it as being an excellent new introduction. My advice is always to seek guidance from other fuchsia growers. If possible take your plant to show it to as many growers as possible – when they are gathered together at a national show would be an excellent opportunity. Continue to grow it for a prolonged length of time before releasing it on to the general market.

List of Sports and Mutations

This is a list of some of the sports or mutations that are available today.

Sport	From
Barrys Queen	Border Queen
Cardinal Farges	Abbé Farges
Carmen Maria	Leonora
Checkers	Checkerboard
Checkmate	Checkerboard
Cloth of Gold	Souvenir de Chiswick
Constance	Pink Pearl
Golden La Campanella	Campanella
Golden Lena	Lena
Golden Marinka	Marinka
Golden Swingtime	Swingtime
Heidi Weiss	Heidi Ann
Herbe de Jacques	Corallina
Lady Thumb	Tom Thumb
Lilian Lampard	Marin Glow
Lorna Doone	General Monk
Nina Wills	Forget me Not
Ornamental Pearl	Cloverdale Pearl
Pixie	Graf Witte
Rose Churchill	Winston Churchill
Rosecroft Beauty	Snowcap
Son of Thumb	Tom Thumb
Spring Bells	Snowcap
Trewince Twilight	Marin Glow
White Ann	Heidi Ann
White Pixie	Pixie

The finding of a sport is the result of careful cultivation. By regularly handling the plants and tending them, the changes in flower or leaf will become noticed. It is as a result of these mutations or sports that we now have double flowers and plants with white corollas, thus we must all keep our eyes open in the hope of finding something new and perhaps an even greater variation in colour or form.

5

Pests and Diseases

Fuchsias are not troubled with a great many pests and diseases. The few that they do suffer are quite easily controlled but of course it is far better not to allow such conditions to really get hold. Prevention is better than cure is a very easy thing to say but there is a great deal of truth in it. One of the most important suggestions always made to beginners to growing fuchsias is not to grow too many plants. Unfortunately this is easier said than done when you have such a wealth of glorious plants from which to choose. However, the advice is valid in that with fewer plants it is possible to handle each of them regularly, and any pests or diseases can be detected at a very early stage.

PESTS

Greenfly

Greenfly can usually be seen in clusters around the light green tip of each shoot, and are unmistakable in appearance. They are sap sucking insects and this action causes distortion and curling of the young leaves. They are very prolific in their reproductive habits so quick action is advisable. Regular spraying with an insecticide such as Tumblebug or Spray Day will keep the greenfly at bay, but I must stress the word regular. There are many old-fashioned remedies for dealing with this pest – if you know of one, and it seems to work well for you, then continue to use it.

Whitefly

Whitefly are extremely troublesome and unfortunately the fuchsia seems to be a particular favourite of this pest. They are easily seen by looking under the upper leaves of plants – the white flies are quite visible. Again they can be controlled by spraying, but unfortunately the sprays are only effective against the adult flies. The eggs are not affected by the sprays

102

so it is necessary to keep spraying at intervals of about four days in order to destroy the newly emerging adults before they can lay further eggs. If a four day spraying programme is carried out even a severe infection can be eradicated in a couple of weeks. The earlier a possible invasion by whiteflies is discovered the easier it will be to eradicate them – so remember to inspect the plants regularly. When there are only a couple of flies a finger and thumb technique is perfectly satisfactory and very satisfying.

Red Spider

Red spider mites are one of the worst pests for fuchsias. They are very difficult to detect in the early stages and are, in fact, almost invisible with the naked eye throughout their life span. Plants which have been attacked by the red spider mite, which is really not a spider at all, can be recognised as the foliage turns to a bronzy colour and becomes very brittle. In later stages very fine webs can be seen spreading from leaf to leaf. This pest is very contagious and rapidly spreads to many plants in a greenhouse.

It is often considered that an attack of red spider mite results from poor growing conditions. The mite thrives in a hot dry atmosphere so if your plants are growing in the ideal warm and moist conditions then they are unlikely to suffer severe attacks. Plants which are affected should be isolated and thoroughly sprayed with a good systemic insecticide. All plants in the greenhouse should be sprayed regularly.

Capsid Bug

Plants which are growing outside can often be attacked by another pest which causes disfiguration and blindness of the growing tips, the capsid bug. This is another sap sucking insect which punctures the young leaves, causing them to blister and turn red. Spraying with insecticide will again cure the condition. Unfortunately it is easy to forget the possibility of plants which are bedded out in the garden being attacked, but it very often happens, especially if the plants are bedded under, or in close proximity to, larger trees.

Vine Weevil

Finally, one pest which seems to have become far more prevalent in recent years (a prevalence which seems to co-incide with the advent of peat-based composts), is the vine weevil larva. The adult is a black beetle-like insect and is nocturnal in its habits. The first sign of the presence of the adult vine weevil is when notches have been eaten from the edge of leaves. At first it is tempting to blame caterpillars. The greatest damage, though, is done not by the adult beetle but by the larvae. The eggs are laid in the surface of the compost and when hatched they produce a grub which is about half an inch (1cm) in length, whitish with a brownish head. These grubs burrow down into the compost and feed off the young white roots, an action which can do untold damage to a young plant.

Many cures are suggested for vine weevils but Malathion soaked into the compost seems to be very effective. The potting back of older plants in the early spring is a good time to discover whether any grubs are present. Again prevention is better than cure – as the adults are nocturnal, they need hiding places by day and rubbish under the staging of greenhouses is very much to their liking.

DISEASES

Botrytis

Botrytis is very easily identified by the grey, rather hairy mould it produces. It can be caused by rather dank airless conditions, the rotting of dying foliage, and general lack of air circulation. The temptation to grow too many plants too closely packed together promotes the conditions for the growth of this disease. The cure is to provide good circulation of air (with vents open throughout the year if possible), and to prevent cold, damp, stagnant conditions. If plants are affected by botrytis then they should be sprayed with a good systemic fungicide or, if the weather is cold and this would only add to the damp conditions, dusting with a fungicide powder.

Rust

Fuchsia rust is another disease which has become far more noticeable in recent years. It is a very debilitating disease and is very easily transmitted from one plant to another. It is readily identified by reddish-brown markings (rings) on the upper side of leaves, and on the underside the typical orangey brown pustules can be seen. As its name suggests, it gives the plant a rusty appearance.

Unfortunately the spores on the underside of the leaves can be passed from one plant to another purely by the movement of air currents. They can also be passed on on the hands of the grower or by insects. The cure for an attack of rust is firstly to isolate any infected plants. Try to remove any of the leaves which have the tell tale marks and *burn* them. The whole plant should then be sprayed with a good fungicide such as Nimrod T or Plantvax 75 if you can get hold of it. Keep the treated plants separate from others and keep a very careful eye on all plants, removing any affected leaves as soon as the first signs show. Unfortunately plants bearing the spores are sometimes first brought into greenhouses from the collections of others. It is a wise precaution to place any newly bought plants in quarantine for a couple of weeks and thus make sure they are not affected. At one stage the complete burning of any affected plant would have been advised but modern teaching is not quite so drastic.

I have talked generally within this chapter of spraying your affected plants with a suitable insecticide or fungicide, but this is not the only method of removing the offending pests or diseases. In fact it would be unwise to use wet sprays on your plants when they are in full flower, as the sprays would cause considerable marking and damage to the flowers and buds. I would always recommend using wet sprays at the beginning of the season before buds are well formed and at the end of the season when plants have been prepared for their winter rests.

Always read the instructions very carefully before mixing your sprays. Follow the instructions and do not think that if you use a spray stronger than that recommended you will get better results – you will only be wasting money and could easily damage the foliage of the plants. As most of the sprays only affect the adult pests, undertake a programme of spraying at intervals of three or four days until the infestation has been cleared. Most pests hide themselves under the leaves of the plants, so ensure that all parts of the plants are well moistened. If the spray you are using is a systemic variety it will give prolonged protection from pests or diseases as the chemical is absorbed through the leaves of the plant and remains in the sap. I would always recommend using a systemic type insecticide or fungicide if one is available.

It is also possible now to obtain insecticide 'pins'. These are pushed into the soil at the base of the plant and the chemical is absorbed by the root system. This is especially useful when the plants are in flower or if you have just a few special plants for show purposes. Although I have not, as yet, tried this method I am assured that it is very successful.

Smoke bombs, or cones, contain a fungicide or insecticide which is released as a cloud of smoke when ignited. These again are very effective at the time of the year when flowers or buds are present but it does mean closing the greenhouse and making it as airtight as possible to prevent the escape of the smoke before the cure has been effected. At the time of the year when we will most need this the days are likely to be hot and all the ventilation possible is usually being given to the plants. However, if it is possible to carry out this smoking last thing at night it should be most effective, and will prevent the necessity of opening the greenhouse door before it has really worked. During damp cold days in late autumn or early winter, when the atmosphere is heavily laden with moisture and we are anxious not to increase the level of dampness in the greenhouse by spraying, then this method of curing the ills is most useful.

Taking the same idea a stage further, it is possible to fix up fumigators or vaporisers in your greenhouse. These are rather more expensive but are extremely effective.

6

Fuchsia Calendar

JANUARY

It is tempting at this time of the year to sit back and think that everything is fine. But do not be lulled into a false sense of security – plants will still need to be looked at to ensure that all is well. January is probably the severest of all months, especially to those plants which have been stored for the winter. See that all protective material is still in position, especially if no heat is being used in your place of storage. If the opportunity presents itself remove the plants from their store and examine them carefully. Do not allow the compost in the pots, or round the roots if stored in boxes, to become bone dry. A little moisture added now will keep the roots alive although growth up above is to be discouraged. Remove any debris that there may be around the plants.

Towards the end of the month, if you require early plants and are able to provide some heat, you will be able to stimulate those plants into fresh life. It will be necessary, though, to provide a good steady heat so don't start them into growth until absolutely necessary.

If you are providing heat throughout the winter then your summer or autumn struck cuttings will be continuing to grow steadily. Don't be tempted to give them too much heat or you will, as a result of the lack of light intensity, have plants which are rather straggly and drawn. These young plants need to be kept growing slowly in a temperature of 45 degrees Fahrenheit (7°C). Do not feed young plants at this time of the year even if they are looking a little pale and wan.

Examine these young plants carefully for any pests or diseases that might be present – remember that as you are providing conditions conducive to plant growth you will also be supplying conditions loved by pests, and they will multiply. Spraying at this time of the year is not recommended, so take care of the pests by using smoke cones, or insecticide sticks, so that the atmosphere remains dry. Remove any leaves which have died or are yellowing. A dead leaf falling across a branch could lead to the loss of the whole branch.

During this month it is quite possible to get bright sunny days. The air will remain cold, but the sun shining through the glass will raise the temperature inside the greenhouse quite considerably. As often as possible open the door and vents so that there is a healthy flow of air. Good air ventilation will help to prevent botrytis. If you do open all your windows, remember to close them again early in the afternoon so that the temperature within the house does not fall too dramatically. An investment in automatic ventilators really repays itself at this time of the year.

On such a bright sunny day, examine the plants that are still out in the garden. The crown of each plant should have been protected with peat, well weathered ashes, bracken or some such other insulation in the autumn. Ensure that this is still in position and renew it if necessary.

During the many inclement days which are experienced during this month, take the opportunity of giving some thought to the situation regarding the materials you will require during the coming season. In the comfort of your sitting room you can look through the gardening magazines and plan for the future. On a bright day you could ensure that the pots and trays you have in store are in a good clean condition and ready for use. Supplies of compost should be considered and ordered if necessary. Supplies of labels, canes, pots, ties, insecticides, fungicides, and feeds should be examined and lists made for ordering when possible. Write off to suppliers of plants for their catalogues and send in your orders as soon as possible to ensure that you stand a better chance of getting what you want.

January is a dismal month really, but it is one full of dreams and promises for the future.

FEBRUARY

Beware this month – promises of things to come one day can be removed with a vengeance the following day. We can expect to have periods of good sunny days when the temperature will soar, especially in the greenhouse, and then, with clear skies during the night the temperature will plummet. Damp weather plus heavy falls of snow can be expected so be prepared, if you are heating your house, to provide the equipment to maintain the required temperature.

Plants overwintering in an unheated position should be

examined carefully at the beginning of the month to ensure that they are still in good condition. Do not allow the compost to become bone dry but add a little moisture to that area when conditions permit. Towards the end of the month it might be necessary to provide some heat to start those plants into growth. Consider partitioning off a small part of a greenhouse which you will be able to heat to a higher temperature. If this proves possible, take your resting plants out of storage, tidy them up slightly by cutting back some of the straggly wood, place them in a warm position and spray overhead with water. This spraying will encourage the young dormant shoots in the leaf axils to soften up and start to grow. Only slight additional watering to the root ball is necessary at this time.

With the production of the young shoots in the axils you will be able to cut back the top growth and start the shaping of your plants. Protect these plants, especially the young shoots, from any severe drop in the temperature that might occur at night. Sheets of newspaper over the plants will help to trap the heat and will protect them. Remove the newspaper by day so that they will receive the maximum amount of light possible. Conversely though, on extremely bright sunny days, which are not unknown in February, keep the plants shaded from the extreme brightness. Ventilation is again of paramount importance. Ventilate as often as the opportunity arises, keeping a flow of air passing through the greenhouse on bright days.

Young plants from summer and autumn cuttings will be growing apace now. Give them as much light as possible, and don't overheat. Try to handle and examine each plant regularly. Those plants which are being grown for bushes should have their growing tips removed as soon as they have reached the required length (usually two or three pairs of leaves). Plants growing as standards should be allowed to grow upright – make sure that a split cane is in position and that the growing whip is tied to it between each pair of leaves. Remove any side shoots that form in the lower leaf axils at an early stage. Keep an eye open for pests and diseases, spray if necessary on dry days but do this as early in the day as possible so that there is not an excess of moisture around when frosts return at night. Examine the root balls of these young plants – if they have filled their pots with roots, pot on into the next sized pot. Do not overfeed, but a feed of perhaps quarter strength might be appreciated. As you handle the plants examine the labels – any which are becoming faint should be replaced.

Make sure you are ready for the cutting season, checking that your propagator is in good working order or that you have sufficient propagators for your purposes. Cuttings taken at the end of this month will provide excellent plants for show work in 3½ inch (9cm) or 5 inch (13cm) pots later in the season.

If you failed to do so last month, make sure your order is sent off to your specialist fuchsia nurseryman. Remember, though, that it is better to see the young plants that you are buying rather than to depend upon a postal service. If you have the chance therefore, collect your plants. Most nurseries are open for business at this time of the year and good young plants will be available which could form the basis of your show plants in the coming season.

If you can get out into the garden, examine the crowns of any plants which are overwintering there. If any of the protective material has been removed (wind and birds can do this) then replace it. Do not expect to see any growths coming up from the base just yet. In spite of your desire to have a meticulous garden do not be tempted to cut back the old, dead, top growth yet – leave that until there are signs of new life from below, as it does protect from the severest frosts. Replace the old labels if necessary.

MARCH

This is the month for which we have all been waiting. It does not matter what the weather is like outside – spring is here (well almost), and life is beginning to return to everything. Starting work now will ensure that you get the real benefit from all those old plants which have been stored through the winter. Prune back some of the top growth, and give them regular overhead sprays with tepid water. Keep them in the warmest place you can find (in the light) and encourage those little pink buds to appear from the leaf axils. Protect them from severe overnight frosts but give them as much light as possible by day.

When the young shoots appear prune back hard so that you are down to one or two shoots on each branch. Repot when they are showing this sign of growth, into a pot a size or two smaller than the one from which they have been taken. Remove all the old compost – wash it off if necessary – and repot using fresh compost, having trimmed back any old and gnarled roots that there may be. Keep the plants in warm and humid conditions to help them recover from this shock. Keep an eye open when repotting for the larvae of the vine weevil, as failure to spot them now might well mean that the new young roots of your plants will become a feast for them later on.

If plants look dead when you take them out of stock, test the bark by gently scraping the surface. If there is green tissue under the bark the plant is still alive; if it is brown then the possibility is that that branch is dead. Test all of the branches before finally discarding the plant.

When suitable shoots are available start taking cuttings – label them carefully and don't take too many, unless you wish to pass them on to friends. Cuttings which were taken last month might need potting into their first individual pots.

Keep a check on your stocks of compost, pots and labels, as nothing is more infuriating than to run out when in the middle of an operation. Also keep a check on the space you are using in the greenhouse – if it is too full now, you will have insufficient space when the plants really start growing.

Keep a very careful eye open for the signs of pests and diseases taking over. Try to get into the habit of carrying out a regular pattern of spraying. Action taken now will keep you trouble-free later. Spray regularly but vary the spray you use, alternating with different types of insecticide so that pests and diseases don't become immune to any one type. Keep all vents open all day, unless frost is still threatening – as much air as possible circulating will help to keep the plants free from moisture-loving diseases such as botrytis.

Towards the end of the month, with the sun rising higher in the sky each day, it will be necessary to consider shading the plants from direct sunlight. There are a number of substances that can be painted on the glass and they are very successful for this purpose. You can invest in a sophisticated blind system if you so wish.

Keep a special watch on those plants that you are training to various shapes. The standard whips need to be kept growing straight and true, and regular neat tying is a necessity. Keep rubbing out the shoots in the leaf axils until you are approaching the height you require. Do not remove the leaves from the trunk until you have built up a very good head on your plant. Bush and shrub trained plants should be turned regularly and the growing tips pinched out to encourage good bushy plants – every two or three pairs of leaves will be sufficient. If you want plants for enjoyment as opposed to show then two stops will be sufficient for your purposes. Plants for baskets should be growing apace. Keep them in their 3½ inch (9cm) pots, pinching them out at three pairs of leaves on each branch. Make sure that your baskets are ready for planting up – the sooner you can do this the sooner they will become established. As often as possible – on good balmy March days – place your plants outside in the fresh air. They will enjoy it.

Examine the bases of your outdoor plants. No shoots will be expected yet. Make sure that any protective material is still in position, and prepare the ground for planting out your new bed of hardies. Don't put them out yet – they should be growing strongly in their pots under cover – as this will not be done until June.

This is a busy month, and there seems to be always something to do. But it is the most important month of the year – get things right now and you are set for a good season.

APRIL

Spring has really arrived now but do not be lulled into a false sense of security, as it is still possible to have very cold nights and cold days. Remember that the north of the country is really two or three weeks behind the south.

Your plants, with the light intensifying each day, will be growing well and the sun shining through the glass can cause quite a dramatic rise in the temperature in the greenhouse. Try to maintain a higher humidity in the greenhouse now by spraying water on the floor and between the pots. Take care with the watering of your plants, as they will rapidly dry out if the temperature soars. If you have not put shading on the glass do so now – or fix blinds.

Make sure that your outside frame is ready to receive plants – clear away any old pots and debris, freshen the surface of the soil, give a thorough soaking with a disinfectant such as Jeyes Fluid, but leave the frame light off and do not attempt to place any plants inside until the fumes have cleared. The frame will be used at the end of the month for hardening off plants which are destined for the open border.

Keep a very careful eye on the way your plants are growing. Try to handle each pot every day – this will tell you if the plant requires watering. Treat each plant as an individual as they will not all require watering at the same time. Regularly turn each plant so that no one side has more of the sun than any other. Keep pinching out the growing tips when two or three pairs of leaves have formed. Standard whips should be reaching the height you require fairly soon. Stop removing the side shoots as they approach this height, as these shoots will be required for the head of the plant.

Watch out for pests and diseases, and continue a regular spraying pattern. Feeding will need to take priority – regular feeding on a little and often basis will give good strong healthy plants which are evenly grown. At this time of the year both top and root growth need building up, so a feed containing a higher proportion of nitrogen is ideal, such as Chempak No. 2 or Vitafeed 3–0–1.

Plants growing strongly in 3½ inch (9cm) or 5 inch (13cm) pots needed for bedding display can be hardened off in the cold frame towards the end of the month. Give them as much air as possible, although the lights should be left in position at the start. After a week or two the lights can be removed during warm days especially if warm April Showers become frequent. At night make sure that the lights are in position and, if frost is threatened, give the added protection of sheets of newspaper over the plants inside the frame. Some growers line their frames with polystyrene ceiling tiles early in the season as insulation. If very severe frosts are forecast then heavier insulation on the frame might be necessary. Some plants, if suffering from the cold, take on a distinctly blue hue on the leaves.

If you are without a greenhouse and have been storing your plants in boxes, in the garage, or have even buried them in the ground, the beginning of this month is the ideal time for you to examine them and start to bring them back to life. Clean them off completely and take them into the warmth of the house and the light of a window. Try to encourage the side shoots to form by regular spraying (mind the furniture), and keep turning them – several times a day if necessary. Once the shoots have started to show, completely remove each plant from its pot and repot into fresh compost. Keep an eye open for any aphids that might have overwintered with your plants. Once good strong fresh growth has been started get the plants into the fresh air as often as you can.

If not already done make sure that your hardy border is prepared for your plants. Dig deeply incorporating some manure and work in a handful or so of bone meal to each square yard. Remember that once the plants are in position they will remain in situ for a number of years. Don't stint on this preparation or you may regret it in a few years.

Make up your baskets but keep them in the greenhouse, standing on large pots on the staging, and only take them outside when the weather is very mild. Keep pinching out the growing tips when three pairs of leaves have been formed. (Remember when you start removing growing tips you must remove *all* of those that can be seen.) Any flowers which form now should be removed, as they are not really true to form and will only serve to weaken the plants.

MAY

Everything is now growing rapidly and it is a job keeping up with all the tasks that present themselves. Some flowers are beginning to appear on the earliest plants. Keep a record of these early-flowering plants so that in future years should an early display be required then the right type of plants can be grown.

All of the overwintered plants should be growing well now and the potting back process should have been completed. If you were troubled with vine weevil make a resolution to keep the area under the staging as clear as possible so that the beetles have nowhere to hide during the day. Keep a very careful eye open for any pests and diseases, and continue to spray regularly with both an insecticide and a fungicide.

Examine any recently purchased plants. It is better to segregate them from your main collection until you are sure that they are clear of diseases. Be on the lookout particularly for signs of rust on your plants. This is noticed first as small brown marks on the upper surface of leaves, then the tell-tale orange coloured pustules are seen underneath. Remove any infected plants, dispose of the affected leaves and spray thoroughly with a good fungicide. Dip the whole plant, including the pot, in a solution of this fungicide to be completely safe. Watch carefully for any signs of a return of the rust on that plant and others which were in its vicinity.

Days are now getting longer, the sun higher, and the temperature more consistent. Do not be tempted to remove all the heat from your houses, especially at night, as the beginning of the month can be treacherous. Keep an eye on the weather forecast each evening and if the night temperature is forecast at 4 degrees centigrade or less keep the heat on. By day keep all vents and doors open so that air can circulate freely. On hot days try to keep a humid atmosphere by spraying the pathways and the benches. This will help to keep the temperature down. Examine the shading that you painted on the glass. It will probably require an extra coating now.

In the border remove any of the winter protection that is still in position. Examine the bases of the plants carefully, and with luck new growths will be starting to show. If the winter has been mild and shoots are appearing on the upper parts of the branches do not be tempted to leave them as you will only have rather unsightly bare stems lower down on your plants. Encourage growth from as low down as possible by cutting back the old wood now, so that only a couple of shoots are left on each branch. A good mulch of well-rotted farmyard manure or a sprinkling of bone meal around the base of each plant will help the plant to build up a good structure for the coming season. Remember that through the season it will be beneficial to give these plants a regular feeding of your usual liquid fertilizer.

Plants hardening off in the cold frame for planting out should be moved into 5 inch (13cm) pots if they have filled their present pots with roots. Do not be tempted, even in the south, to plant out your hardies until the very end of this month or the beginning of next. Plant deeply when you do – a couple of inches below the level of the compost in the pot is ideal.

Keep up a regular pattern of feeding your plants – this applies to pot plants and border plants. A feeding at dilute strength every time you water will be beneficial. Do not feed a plant that is ailing, rather discover the cause of the discontent and correct this before feeding. A plant that has been suffering at the roots for any reason could benefit by foliar feeding.

Continue to pinch out the growing tips of the plants if you want bushy plants for a specific date, but bear in mind that you need to leave eight weeks for single flowered varieties and ten weeks for double flowered plants before they will come into flower. At the beginning of this month it might not be a bad idea to look at the show dates and work backwards from there to ascertain the last possible date upon which you should pinch out your plants. The times given are only a general guide – depending on prevailing weather conditions you may require longer.

Continue to train the heads of your standards, trying to get them as evenly shaped as you possibly can. Consider the size of pot that they are in. Usually standards of the larger types, the half standards and the full standards, can be shown in any size of pot. If they become pot bound, that is if the roots completely fill the pots, at any stage of their growth, the standards will want to flower. The possibility of shaping the head well diminishes as soon as flower buds start to appear.

Thinking ahead to next year, if the conditions that you are able to offer your plants during the winter are conducive to continuous steady growth, then you might consider growing some plants on the biennial method. Briefly, this is growing the plants one year and flowering them the next. You will require a minimum temperature of 40–45 degrees Fahrenheit (7–8°C) to be maintained throughout the winter, which could be costly. However, the larger plants you see on the show bench are grown by this method. You will need to take cuttings now if plants are to be grown in this way. Soft tip cuttings are the best to use and they can be as small as you like. Choose only those varieties that you wish to have on the show bench. They will need no bottom heat for rooting and can be treated quite severely throughout their initial growth. If cuttings have rooted before the end of this month pot them into small pots, 3 inch (7½cm) pots would be ideal, and let them grow on steadily. It will be necessary to start the training of these plants at a very early stage. Within a few weeks of rooting, when two pairs of leaves have been formed, the growing tips should be removed. The branching process will have started. These plants will not be allowed to flower this year.

JUNE

This is the time for considering planting out into the permanent beds. The well-prepared beds should be marked out ready for receiving the plants. The hardy plants should have been well hardened off by now in the cold frame and the majority will have been in 5 inch (13cm) pots. It is better to plant in groups of three of the same cultivar. Plant these permanent bedders deeply, removing them from their pots and planting so that the top surface of the compost is approximately 2 inches (5cm) beneath the surface of the soil. Remove the plants from the pots even if the intention is to take them back inside for protection during the winter. It is far better to leave them out, having prepared the garden well – even if the cultivars chosen are not considered to be hardy, give them the chance. Before planting out make sure of the heights to which your plants could grow. Placing the tallest at the back and the shortest in the front will give a good picture. Consider using standards as dot plants but remember that they must not stay out over the winter.

Plants growing as biennials will be growing well. Continue to pinch out all growing tips at every second pair of leaves. You must make sure that each growing tip is removed to get a symmetrical plant. These plants are stronger and grow sturdier if they are grown without the protection of glass throughout the summer. If you have an area where grass is allowed to grow then place your plants in this environment to maintain the moistness that they like so much. When outside keep a very careful eye open for pests and spray regularly. The capsid bug on outdoor plants is a nuisance as it causes distortion of the young growing tips.

Plants in the greenhouse will need heavy shading all the time now. Keep the vents and doors open day and night so that there is a constant stream of air through each plant. Damp down the floors and benches daily. Allow plenty of space between plants on the benches – they should not be touching each other. Continue to turn the plants (perhaps a quarter turn daily) so that there is even growth. When the first flower buds appear, perhaps towards the end of the month, let them flower if you require your plants purely for decorative purposes, or remove the flower buds if you are timing them for a specific show. Don't forget the length of time necessary from the final pinch to getting the plant in full flower. Some growers remove all flowers which are out until fourteen days before the show and then let them flower.

Keep an eye on your baskets and half baskets which can now be placed outside permanently. Remember that they will require daily attention for watering and feeding. Keep an eye open for pests, especially the white fly – early treatment will prevent a major epidemic. You can, if you wish, continue to take cuttings. These could be useful to grow on as biennial plants, retained in 3½ inch (9cm) pots during the winter, but it is often found that cuttings taken during these hottest months are less easy to root. Loss of moisture both from the compost and as a result of transpiration prevents rapid rooting. The coolest spot combined with some method of maintaining high humidity around the cuttings is the answer.

117

Continue the regular feeding – fuchsias are gross feeders and will repay your efforts. It might not be a bad idea now to change to a feed with a different analysis – Chempak No. 3 is recommended for this time of the year as it is a balanced food of equal proportions of nitrogen, potash and phosphates.

More and more flowers will be appearing as the month progresses. Keep a record of the dates so that plans can be made for future years. Enjoy the flowers and invite others in to see them so that they too can share your enjoyment – any spare rooted cuttings will make delightful gifts. Visit the greenhouses of other growers and try to visit as many nurseries as you can so that you can make a wider choice for another year. Don't rely on memory – make a note of the cultivars that you have seen and admired.

JULY

This is the time of the year to work towards. It doesn't really matter if you are growing plants with the intention of showing them or whether you grow them purely for the pleasure they give, flowers are everywhere. It is possible now to go round to other people's gardens, nurseries and fuchsia shows and admire the immense wealth of colour and beauty of form. If you haven't started keeping a note book keep one now. Don't let the name of a plant you admire escape you.

Keep a keen eye on your own plants and take off all old flowers as soon as they begin to look a little jaded. Remove any foliage that is becoming exhausted – one leaf falling across a branch could easily spoil the whole plant. The more flowers you remove the more you will get, as the plant tries to form seeds to ensure the continuation of the species. If you do not allow the seed to form more will have to be made.

Towards the end of the month the show scene will be getting into full swing. Visit as many as you can – with your note book. Visit the Society table and if there are any queries you have about any aspect of fuchsia growing do not be afraid to ask – you will find the officials only too pleased to oblige. If you are doubtful about the name of a plant you have in your collection take along a twig of it containing flowers, buds and foliage, as it is just possible somebody might recognise it.

If you are entering plants in the shows make sure your entry form arrives with the show secretary in plenty of time. This is the key to successful showing – take plenty of time. Never be rushed into doing something, whether it is arriving at the show venue or arranging your plants on the benches. It has taken a long time to produce your show plant, so present it to its best possible advantage. Any canes or ties you use to support branches that are heavily laden with flowers should be as inconspicuous as possible. Make sure that they are pest free. Use insecticide pins or a systemic insecticide watered into the compost – do not spray open flowers or well developed buds as they will be severely stained. Any powder residues from feeds you may have used should be carefully removed from the leaves. A final spray with clear water when the plants are staged will give them a sprightly look. Examine all your plants carefully before leaving them, in an effort to find those seed pods hiding amongst the foliage. If possible get someone else to look for you as well – two pairs of eyes are better than one.

If you are really adventurous, and have the space, now is the time to be thinking of hybridising. It should be easy to choose the plants you wish to use as parents, as they will be showing off the desired characteristics now. But be patient and don't expect instant success.

Continue with regular feeding both inside and outside the greenhouse. Take care with the watering, remembering that water droplets on leaves and flowers will magnify the sun's rays shining through the glass and will cause unsightly scorch marks. Continue to try and handle each plant daily. Make a note of any idiosyncracies that you may see amongst your plants – some need more feed or root space than others, or object to being severely pinched. If a certain plant does not seem to want to grow for you, in spite of the fact that it grows like a weed next door, do not despair, as you can try again next year if you wish or, far better, give that plant a miss and grow those which do really well for you.

Cuttings will root now if you need them but the higher outside temperature is not really conducive to quick rooting. Leave it until next month or even the month after when you will be in more control of the propagating temperature.

Plants out in the garden will now be in full bloom. If you have planted them too closely together this will now be easily noticeable. Keep an eye open for any pests and diseases that may be lurking out there and deal with them before they become too severe. Pick off dead flowers and seed pods to ensure continuous flowering. Be ready to stop and chat to admirers when you are tending your beautiful plants in the front garden.

AUGUST

It is a real pleasure to be able to walk in the garden or the greenhouse at this time of the year, with everything in full flower. Shows are in full swing – every weekend there is another show or two that can be visited. Take the opportunity, as the season is short, and don't forget that record you need to keep of the cultivars that attract you – they might not have attracted the judges but that is of little importance.

The plants in the garden will welcome a regular boost of a liquid feed. Don't forget the plants in the hanging baskets – they will need regular attention to make sure that they do not completely dry out (a soaking in a bucket of water will be beneficial). Remove all spent flowers, seed pods and yellowing leaves. If plants are looking a little sickly, examine them carefully as it could be an infection of red spider mite or green fly. Yellowing of the leaves may be a result of magnesium deficiency, and a dose of Epsom salts (magnesium sulphate) will soon redress the balance.

Any flowers that you pollinated last month might be getting to the stage when the ripe berries will fall, so watch them carefully. If you successfully obtain some seed sow it straight away. If you intend to keep a section of your greenhouse heated during the winter then cuttings taken now will grow steadily and produce some excellent plants for next year – you will need good, well formed plants for planting out and in the baskets, so this might be worth considering. A minimum of 40 degrees Fahrenheit (7°C will keep them just ticking over.

Plants which are growing on the biennial method will be standing outside in 4 inch (10cm) or 5 inch (13cm) pots. Don't be tempted to pot them on into larger pots even if the present pots are filled with roots. Don't allow them to flower, but keep pinching out the growing shoots and feed them with a high nitrogen fertilizer. Remove them from the pots and cut off the lowest part of the root ball before replacing with some fresh compost to keep the root system active. Make sure that these plants are kept pest free.

At this time of year many people are growing their fuchsias in tubs on their patios. If one really catches your eye find out what different types of plants have been used to build up the display. If it is possible, obtain some cuttings of the plants used for foliage as they are likely to root quite easily at this time of year. Use other plants to complement your fuchsias.

SEPTEMBER

The plants should still be looking fine, perhaps a little jaded in their pots but after a busy season they are in need of a rest. All plants should really be outside at this time of year, so stand all of the pot plants outside to help the shoots to ripen in preparation for the winter.

Plants growing in the garden are probably looking better now than they have ever done. This could be because of the heavy dews experienced during this month, or the extra humidity around them. Most plants will be showing signs of new fresh growth – the tips of the branches will be looking a fresher green colour and new flower buds will be forming. This second flush of growth can be of use to us, both from the decorative point of view in the garden and also in providing us with new cutting material.

Cuttings can still be taken, in fact this might be considered to be the ideal time to take them to have good young plants growing away well at the very beginning of next season. Cuttings taken now will not require the assistance of any heat to root, in fact I usually place them under the staging of the greenhouse away from the bright sun. These rooted cuttings can be allowed to develop in the late autumn and then kept ticking over during the winter. They don't take up a great deal of space. When taking the cuttings try to remove the small buds in the tips without damaging the growing shoots.

Continue to feed all of the plants. A feed containing a high potash content will be beneficial now. Chempak No.4 is ideal, as is Phostrogen. This high potash content will help to ripen up the wood. It is not really advisable to pot on plants at this stage unless you can be sure that they will make a good root system around the new compost.

Watch carefully for pests and diseases. Regular spraying or the use of insecticide pins and systemic insecticides will help to keep them in check. It is very easy at this stage of the season to forget this important task. Pests which escape your notice now might well overwinter amongst the plants, ready to start a fresh invasion in the spring.

Continue to remove all dead flowers and seed pods. Don't be tempted to use these seed pods as seeds – you will know the parentage of the seed bearing plant but will not know the pollen bearer. It would be pure luck if you obtained anything really worthwhile and a lot of space and energy will have been used up. Make sure that any dying leaves are removed from the plants as botrytis could easily set in, helped by the moist conditions that are prevailing now.

Give some thought towards the end of the month to the winter storage of your plants. With everything out of your greenhouse, on a bright sunny day, give your greenhouse a thorough cleaning out, as cleanliness now will pay dividends later. Plan your winter storage – if you have too many of certain cultivars decide which you will dispose of. Friends will still be pleased to receive them.

OCTOBER

The evenings are now drawing in, the night dew is even heavier and the plants in the garden are blooming well. This is a dangerous month, and one during which we can expect the first frosts. Plants which have been standing outside can continue to do so, but keep an eye on the weather forecast. If frost is threatened then they must go under cover. Actually, no great damage is likely to be done by a slight frost – in fact if anything it might well do a bit of good.

The very youngest plants, especially those which were rooted as cuttings during the last couple of months, will not stand any frost. Their immature shoots are very susceptible to damage, so make sure that they are kept in a warm position. If you have thermostatically controlled heat then it is wise to use this now, to keep a temperature of about 45 degrees Fahrenheit (7°C). A fan heater at this time of year is ideal for keeping the air moving.

Plants out in the garden will probably be continuing to flower profusely – other summer bedding plants will long since have passed their best, but the fuchsias keep going. It is still possible to take those soft tip cuttings if you wish.

You must now decide what you are going to do with your outside plants. You might like to leave them in the garden to give them a chance to show what strength and hardiness they have. It is not a bad idea to make a sketch plan showing where your plants are situated and giving their names, as it is amazing how often labels seem to disappear during the winter. Whilst you can still see the flowers you will still know the names. Any of the more tender varieties that you decide to leave outside should be the main plants from which you take some late cuttings as a simple insurance. If you have used standards for your bedding take them indoors – it would be a pity to lose the plants by virtue of the stem becoming frosted. These plants take up quite a lot of space for storage so special consideration needs to be given.

Plants which were left in their pots during the summer will need to be taken inside later. Don't be in too much of a hurry, as the first frost will not kill them but simply help in the defoliation. Most will probably still be in full flower so take advantage of that bonus. Continue to keep an eye open for pests and remove them by spraying. If you have returned some of the plants to the greenhouse and pests are found it is better to kill them by using smoke cones rather than moisten the atmosphere in the greenhouse too much by spraying.

Some of the Nurserymen will be sending out next season's catalogues so make sure you get your copy. Decide which of the new varieties you have seen this year you wish to add to your collection. If you have sown seeds from the plants that you hybridised, the first successful germinations will be visible. Treat them gently and pot them on as soon as they are large enough to handle. Remember, though, that they are very erratic in their germination so do not throw away the compost from the pot until you are sure that no other seedlings are going to appear – it is always the late arrival which makes the best plant.

NOVEMBER

This is a dangerous month for plants, as many still want to continue to flower although generally they will be showing signs of tiredness. There is no point in trying to force them to continue, rather encourage them to rest.

Reduce the amount of watering you give to plants that are still outside, as the heavy night dews will be all they need. Consider bringing all plants in under cover, but before doing so make sure that your storage area is clean and free from pests. Plants must also be free from pests and diseases so, before bringing them inside remove all the remaining leaves. You may prune back some of the more straggly stems if you wish but do not be tempted to prune too severely. When all foliage has been removed and no debris remains on the surface of the compost, give the whole plant a thorough spraying with a mixture of insecticide and fungicide. Make sure that the plant is thoroughly soaked and give it a chance to dry off slightly before taking it inside. Don't pack the plants together too tightly. Be in a position to give them a covering of some insulating material to protect them from frosts. The method of winter storage is covered fully elsewhere in this book.

Very young plants will need preferential treatment now, requiring a minimum temperature of 45 degrees Fahrenheit (7°C) to keep them just growing. Don't let them grow too fast, as the light intensity is insufficient to give sturdy growth. Keep an eye open for pests and spray if the weather is conducive – on damp misty days when the air is still and almost stagnant, do not attempt to spray.

Biennial plants will be allowed just to tick over. Don't feed or encourage growth. Any leaves which turn yellow and drop off should be removed from the pot. Some will, but do not worry, more will grow to take their places in the spring. Outdoors the hardies will probably continue to flower. Make the most of this but it might be worth putting a protection of peat around the base of the plants at this point. They will probably be looking a bit straggly but don't be tempted to cut them back.

DECEMBER

This is a really quiet month with very little that can be done. Watering, if at all necessary, should be undertaken with the greatest of care, or the atmosphere in the greenhouse will become damp and cold. It is important though that the plants should not be allowed to get bone dry as more plants are lost through this than through excessive watering.

Young plants will be looking a little fed up, perhaps succumbing to the dullness of the weather. Do not worry, if you maintain the minimum heat recommended, with the increase in daylight hours and light intensity from the end of this month things will improve. Still keep an eye open for any pests and deal with them by means of smoke cones. Also keep an eye open for any leaves which fall on to lower branches – remove them or the shape of your plant might be spoilt.

If you want very early cuttings some of your stock plants

can be brought back to life by spraying the branches with tepid water. Place them in the warmest part of the greenhouse. The young shoots which form can be used for the very earliest cuttings at the end of the month. Use them when they have formed just two pairs of leaves and the soft tip – these could be described as ultra green tip cuttings.

During the cold dark evenings, take the opportunity to look back over the past season, to remember the mistakes made and to ensure that they are not repeated. Examine the stored plants regularly and make sure that the compost is not bone dry. Ensure that the protective covering round the base of the hardies is in position and that any dead foliage has been removed from the overhead branches. Send off your renewal form to any societies that you may have joined – the Local Society and the British Fuchsia Society deserve your support.

Sit back, enjoy the rest, browse through catalogues, spend pleasant evenings looking at your coloured slides and dream of the successes to come.

7
Fuchsias for Pleasure

One of the difficulties of writing any book on a specific plant is the temptation to write as though all readers were only concerned with growing plants for the show bench. If that impression has been given in this book then apologies are due. The real intention is to encourage as many people as possible to grow as many different types of fuchsias as they are able, purely and simply for the pleasure that they give. To be successful it is necessary to aim for a certain standard. Plants can be allowed to grow untended and roam freely but no great satisfaction would be achieved from that type of cultivation. The standards that we set are the standards that members of societies aim to achieve on the show bench. We all have marvelled at the magnificent specimens that we have seen and have, secretly perhaps, intended to emulate such feats.

The purpose when growing plants, whether it is for our own pleasure, or because we wish to compare our ability to grow plants with others, is to produce as magnificent a specimen as we possibly can. A bush is not a bush if it is just a single scraggy stem with a few flowers; a standard is not a satisfying standard if it has a crooked stem and an uneven head; a basket is not a spectacle if it is just a few scrawny branches hanging over the edge of a basket. The object of this book therefore is to help anyone interested in growing fuchsias to grow something of which they can be rightly proud. Such plants are not necessarily meant for showing on the show bench – showing off in the garden will suffice.

Putting the show bench to one side then, how can we use our fuchsias to obtain maximum enjoyment? As stated in other chapters it is possible of course to grow them in a flower bed of their own, to have a border especially designed and cultivated for fuchsias. Experiment with all types of plants from the very small creeping plants to the giant standards at the back of the border. Have them growing in troughs along our window-sills, or in pots hanging from the walls; growing in patio tubs; as dot plants in a bed of other annuals. Fuchsias will fulfil all these functions – simply sit back and admire their glorious simplicity.

It is interesting to listen to the comments of friends when they examine plants in a collection, and it is usually obvious when they have seen something that has impressed them. Most seem to appreciate seeing the fuchsia growing naturally, but cultivars must be carefully chosen for this purpose, or the glorious flowers hanging pendulously from the branches will lose most of their glory. Choose strong upright growers which hold their flowers away from the earth. Let the plants grow as high as you can so that they can be easily seen.

A trough on a window-sill is certainly an excellent way in which to display plants – wonderful shows of trailing geraniums can be seen growing from the balconies of houses in Austria. For a trough, concentrate on the type of plants that are low growing and have the tendency to trail over the edge. A good basket variety would suit the purpose very well so the choice is very wide indeed. I prefer to use low growing plants – Tom Thumb, Lady Thumb and Son of Thumb are ideal for this sort of position. Another that would suit admirably is Westminster Chimes, and a smaller basket variety which always does well is Auntie Jinks. A glance through a catalogue will introduce you to many others that would be suitable.

Although whenever shows are discussed we tend to think of fuchsias on their own it would be foolish to do so when growing for display. The fuchsias will complement, and will be complemented by, other low growing plants such as lobelia, allysum, petunia, fibrous begonias and any of the silvery foliage plants that are available. In nature nothing really clashes so it is possible to achieve a variation in colour and texture which will give great satisfaction.

I am very much in favour of hanging pots. It is only quite recently that such a class was permitted in British fuchsia shows, but I predict that their future lies not with the shows but as displays outside houses and bungalows. One of the difficulties when growing a basket of fuchsias, or any other plants, is the weight of the basket when full of moist compost and plants. With the larger baskets a strong and fairly long bracket is required so that the blooms of the plants will not be bruised when the wind blows them against the brickwork. I often wonder whether it would be at all possible for some of the superb baskets seen in shows ever to have seen a bracket outside a house, as they have been grown so successfully that such a position would be impossible. So the hanging pot with its smaller area and weight and shorter bracket is an ideal receptacle for trailing fuchsias.

It is possible to have any number of these along a wall without making it look overdressed and ostentatious. I think that a little care is necessary in choosing the type of plant for this type of pot, as the larger, more flamboyant flowers look rather out of place. There are a number of smaller flowering cultivars that would fill the job admirably and again I would suggest that they can be complemented by using trailing lobelia or allysum or even the smaller trailing geraniums and begonias. It is not necessary to overfill such a pot, as one plant each of three or four types of flowers would be suitable.

Within shows the 14 or 15 inch basket (36 or 38cm) is usually recommended. It is possible to purchase baskets with much smaller diameters – a 10 inch (25cm) basket can give a marvellous show of colour. Your baskets do not need to be made of the traditional wire, modern plastics (with or without saucers attached) are also very useful. But be careful of the colour, as some are rather garish and a more neutral colour will enhance the plants.

It is not necessary to confine yourself to 'proper' baskets or pots – why not make up your own containers? Slatted wooden containers with green moss showing through the bars and plants growing, apparently naturally, through and over them would be very effective. Let your imagination wander so that the container is part of your planning – a search through some of the old junk shops or amongst the stalls at car boot sales will probably produce many containers which will be very suitable.

Bearing in mind the need for height it is possible nowadays to obtain towers for growing such things as strawberries – receptacles with holes cut in the sides into which plants can be grown. These have the advantage of being portable, and a number of different cultivars, grown together to give a pleasing colour effect would create a pillar of flowers. Again, interspersing the fuchsias with other flowers and foliage would only add to the enjoyment.

Plastic downpipes, about 4 inches (10cm) in diameter, with holes cut at regular intervals, and filled with compost, could be the host for a great many plants. You would need to be very careful with the watering and the fixing of the tube of flowers to an upright, but what a spectacle it would be.

Bare walls or fencing can be a rather boring sight on a summer's day but such structures can be used for displaying plants. It is possible to obtain pot holders – simple designs for holding a 5 inch (13cm) pot in position – and these can be attached to the wall or fence and a plant displayed from them. These pot holders were used to great effect at the Stoke on Trent National Garden Festival and were admired by all who saw them. If you have the space and the ability to build yourself a pergola then you have the vehicle upon which many, many fuchsias can be displayed. There is nothing better than looking up into the flower of the fuchsia to obtain its true glory. The pot holders can be fixed on the uprights of the pergola so there will be fuchsias at all heights.

The patio is an area of the garden where the fuchsia can really excel. It is possible these days to purchase, reasonably cheaply, many different sizes, shapes and colours of containers, and you can be as modern or as ancient as you wish. They come in so many different heights that you can really build up a stage upon which the fuchsia can be displayed. It would be nice if more fuchsia societies in their shows encouraged the growing of fuchsias in patio tubs by incorporating a class for them. It is important though not to confine the plants in a tub to one genus. Use as many colour combinations as you can – use lobelia and allysum, begonias and ivy-leaved geraniums, cinneraria and other silver leaved foliage plants and combine them with fuchsias to produce a mass of colour. There can be no better satisfaction than to see someone carefully examining a tub containing a variety of different flowers – every movement of one plant will reveal the glories of another. Use your fuchsias to get height and also use them to cascade over the edge of the container. Consider the plants which have interesting foliage – the *triphylla* types, Tom West, Autumnale (or Burning Bush) or any of the sports which carry golden foliage. They can all be used with great effect.

Having dealt with the decorative ability of the fuchsia outside the house it is worth considering whether fuchsias have a part to play inside. Undoubtedly they do, but it should be remembered that the fuchsia is not really a house plant. In its natural environment the fuchsia receives moisture from the plants around it and needs to have a warm humid atmosphere. The normal conditions which exist in our houses are therefore not really suitable, being too dry. I tend to liken the requirements of the fuchsia with those of the African violet (Saintpaulia). To succeed, a moistness around the foliage is necessary. One solution is to stand the pot on a saucer or tray containing moist gravel. The humidity thus provided will be beneficial to the plants. It is often recommended that African violets and other similar plants enjoy the moister atmosphere in a kitchen or bathroom – perhaps our fuchsias would like a similar situation. Fuchsias may not be house plants, but there is no reason why they should not be used as temporary visitors. A plant in full bloom brought into the dry atmosphere of a living room will give an excellent display for a short period of time but will need to be taken out again to recover its vitality. There have been many complaints over the years that fuchsias purchased at fuchsia shows in late July and August have lost their buds and dropped their leaves when taken indoors. A change of environment, the trauma of being carried from one place to another, the dryness of the atmosphere within a house, the lack of sufficient light, excessive watering – all are factors which need to be taken into consideration. By all means give them a place in the home for a very short time and then give them time to recover.

As table decorations there is nothing to better a miniature standard – as a centre-piece it will be a talking point. At one time the quarter standard was referred to as the table standard but it is safe to say that this title has been taken over by the miniature standard with its 5–10 inch (13–25cm) stem and proportional head. As these little beauties can be grown in one short season it is well worth spending a little time and effort in so doing.

PLANTS IN THE GARDEN

There can be no possible doubt that the best place to see fuchsias growing is in the open garden. They are so useful as bedding plants or as tall dot plants. They can also be used for hedges, and anyone who has had the opportunity of visiting Ireland will have marvelled at the roads lined with tall fuchsia hedges. Fuchsias can be left out in the garden all the year round, indeed there are some cultivars which are extremely hardy and will come up year after year and make a very good display from early in the season.

Many of the modern cultivars, with very attractive colourings, are extremely hardy. I define a hardy fuchsia as one which will remain in the garden throughout the winter, one which will, in the Spring, send up fresh young growth from below the soil level and will produce flowers from the middle to the end of July. If plants survive the winter but fail to produce flowers until much later in the season then they are of little value to us.

It is almost impossible to produce a recommended list of hardy fuchsias, as a great deal will depend upon your own location. In the south of England, or those parts of the country favoured with the warmth of the Gulf Stream, many plants normally considered tender will survive and give an excellent display. My suggestion would therefore be to give your favourite cultivar an opportunity to show you whether or not it is hardy.

Hardy Plant Classification

It is possible to decide whether or not it will be safe to try to grow particular plants as permanent features in the garden simply by studying the descriptions given in the catalogues of specialist fuchsia nurserymen. Within the descriptions you will often see the codes H.1, H.2, and H.3. These codes can be defined as follows:

H.1   requires greenhouse heated to a minimum of 40°F (4 to 5°C)
H.2   requires cool greenhouse – half hardy
H.3   denotes the plant is hardy

Although these are classifications given by nurserymen, it is often found that fuchsias described as H.2 will grow out of doors with excellent results and obviously with bigger blooms than on H.3 plants. As conditions vary so much from place to place – even in different parts of the same garden – it is always worth trying fuchsias outside. The first winter is always the most dangerous time, where the greatest care is needed.

Care of Garden Plants

It is important to give your young plants a good start by preparing the ground thoroughly. Remember that once planted there should be no need to move the plant for a number of years. Dig in a good quantity of well-rotted manure – failing this I would suggest digging in good quantities of peat and a generous amount of a slow acting fertilizer such as bone meal. Fairly deep digging is important as deep planting is recommended. The plants you should use are ones which are growing strongly, preferably in 5 inch (13cm) pots, or at the least in 3½ inch (9cm) pots. The planting out into the open garden will take place at the end of May or the beginning of June so cuttings for these plants will have been taken in autumn or very early spring. The plants should be well developed, bushy, and growing strongly.

As our object should be to get a large mound of flowers, I suggest that you always plant out your young plants in groups of three, four or five. They will grow up strongly together and make an excellent show. Each plant should be about 9 inches (23cm) from its neighbour and a gap of approximately 18 inches (46cm) should be left between groups. The usual recommendation when planting from pots into the garden is that the soil level should be the same as the level of the compost in the pot, but this is not so with fuchsias. I suggest that, as the roots need as much protection as possible in the first winter, plant them deeply so that the surface of the compost in the pot is about two to three inches below the surface of the soil. This can be achieved by making a saucer-shaped indentation in the soil about two inches (5cm) deep, making the hole for the root ball in the centre of this indentation. During the remainder of the summer the saucer shape will gradually fill and the root ball will be at the required level. The plants can then be allowed to develop and flower. If you have started out with good bushy plants there will be no need to carry out any further stopping of the laterals, simply allow the plants to grow naturally and flower continuously – they will amply reward you for all the work put into their planting.

If the autumn is mild it is possible for these plants to continue flowering throughout October, November and into December. Unfortunately we do occasionally have very severe frosts early in the season, which have the effect of stopping the flowering and bringing on the premature defoliation of the plants. The temptation will be to proceed to the garden with secateurs and trim back the bare looking branches. Please don't, as those bare looking branches will give considerable protection from frosts to the base of our plants. Any protection we can give to the roots, particularly during the first winter, will be of inestimable value to the plants.

Additional protection can be given by pulling soil up around the base or by giving added protection with peat or well-weathered ashes. The argument against using peat for this protection is that the moistness held by the peat can freeze solidly and therefore give little protection from frosts. However, I feel that any substance which gives an added blanket around the base of the plants must be of value. Nature often helps by providing, on occasions, a blanket of snow before subjecting us to severe frosts.

With the advent of spring it is certainly very exciting to be able to examine the bases of plants and find fresh young growths pushing their way through. It is only when these fresh young growths are seen that you should consider removing the old stems. They can be cut back very severely so that only a couple of inches (about 5cm) at the most remain above the surface. Occasionally, when we have mild winters, the upper branches of the plants are not killed by the frosts and fresh young growths can be seen breaking out from the branches quite high up. Do not be tempted to reduce your cutting back of these branches – even when the growth is there I would still recommend cutting the stems back almost to ground level. The reason for this is that fuchsias only flower on fresh new growth, they will not flower from the old wood, so if your young branches are coming away from the old wood at a fairly high position there will be quite a length of bare stem at the bottom. This will look very unsightly and not in the least attractive as the season progresses. What is needed is green growth and flowers from as low down on the bushes as possible.

A border of fuchsias can be very attractive indeed but as with all plants, there are some cultivars which grow taller than others. Try to obtain an estimate of the height each group is likely to achieve and plant them so that the taller ones are at the back. There are some very low growing fuchsias which will make extremely good plants for the front of the border. Some that come to mind instantly are the Thumb family, Lady Thumb, Tom Thumb and Son of Thumb. These grow to a height of about a foot (about 30cm) and will make excellent clumps of flowers when planted in small groups. If you are specifically buying plants for planting out permanently, enquire as to their final heights. If you can get hold of a catalogue from a specialist fuchsia grower, an indication of the hardiness and the height will be shown.

In very favoured parts of the country it is possible to grow hedges of fuchsias. These will require the same sort of treatment when planting as already described, but bear in mind that they will be in position for a very long time and will require a very good start.

Plants which are growing in the gardens should be fed, in fact I think it is a good idea to get into a regular pattern of feeding your outdoor plants. A good balanced feed, such as Phostrogen, will be ideal for use throughout the season, once the plants are established. It is also important to carry out a regular spraying programme. Outdoor plants do not suffer to quite the same extent as those under cover – whitefly is less of a nuisance, but it is important to keep an eye open for greenflies. Capsid bugs, especially if your plants are close to trees, can be a nuisance, causing blindness in the young shoots.

A list of recommended cultivars, including those hardy enough for garden use, can be found in Chapter 2.

8

Exhibition Fuchsias

FUCHSIA SHOWS

Without doubt the best place to see fuchsias exhibiting all their beauty is at a fuchsia show. Around the country, from the beginning of July until the middle of September, it is possible to visit a show each weekend. At these shows you will be able to meet people who grow their plants almost with a fanaticism, people who grow their fuchsias for love of the flowers and form and who are prepared to bring along their pride and joy for others to see and admire.

There are a few dedicated growers and showers who will travel from show to show during the season, but they are very limited in number. They are often maligned and called 'pot hunters' – I think this is grossly unfair, as no fortune has ever been made in the showing of fuchsias, in fact the cost of their transportation will most likely leave the grower heavily in debt at the end of the season. Most of these people do this simply for the satisfaction they achieve in pitting their horticultural skills against others with similar interests. But it isn't just the competitive element which is so important, it is also the satisfaction of having worked with nature over a long season to produce something which is as near perfection as possible.

The 'showing' members of any society are prepared to present their plants for general inspection and criticism but they do more than just that, they are there also to help, encourage and guide others to achieve the same skills. When you attend a fuchsia show do not be afraid to ask questions of those who have exhibited – I have no doubt you will be pleasantly surprised at the amount of information that they will offer.

To get the maximum satisfaction out of attending a show it is necessary to know precisely what is being asked for in each of the classes. To this end I suggest that the first thing to do on arriving is to ask for a schedule of the classes. These are usually available, either as separate documents given to each enquirer, or as fixtures at the end of each bench. A schedule is the set of rules which governs the show. Each class is described in detail so that each exhibitor will know precisely what is called for and the judges will be able to compare like with like. These rules must be obeyed absolutely, as failure to do so will result in the letters NAS, being written on the competitors card. NAS stands for 'not according to schedule' and can be used for any one of several reasons. Most classes call for plants to be exhibited in pots of a certain size, and pots exceeding that size will be penalised. Classes call for differing types of growth – hence a standard fuchsia shown in a class calling for bushes would be penalised. Standard fuchsias have to conform to strict measurements with regard to the length of their stems, and so on. It is important therefore that intending competitors read the schedule very closely so that the plants they have nurtured so carefully will be exhibited in the right class.

Once you have your schedule, move around the show starting at the first class and carry on right through to the end. Look at the plants in each class carefully, read what the schedule says about it, and then try to discover why one plant was preferred by the judges to another. If you are completely bemused by their decision, ask. Most judges remain in attendance for a large part of the time that the show is open and will be delighted to explain the reasons behind their decisions. Usually, though, the reasons for the selection of one plant over another will be self evident. At the end of your tour of the show, if you feel that your plants are of the same standard, now is the time to start thinking about next year.

First of all it is important to look at the schedule to discover if it is necessary to belong to the society putting on the show, or whether it is open to any grower. Usually shows are confined to society members, so the first step you will need to take will be to become a member. This is a very simple process and you will probably find a society table at the show, where it is possible to obtain more details or even to sign on there and then. The annual subscriptions of most societies are minimal and the benefits obtained far outweigh the cost. Having taken that first step, you should now examine the schedule in more detail.

The schedule will tell you the size of pot permitted in each class. The usual sizes of pots in which plants are exhibited are 3½ inch (9cm), 5 inch (13cm) or 6 inch (15cm). The reason for restricting the size of the pot is quite simply to restrict the size of the plant being displayed. The amount of root space in a pot will determine the amount of top growth the plant can achieve. It is important that the size of the plant is in proportion to the size of the pot. A huge specimen growth in a 3½ inch pot will be out of proportion and will be seriously downgraded by the judge. It follows of course, that plants in 5 inch pots will be larger than those in 3½ inch pots, and those in 6 inch pots will be even larger.

It is also possible that the schedule will call for plants showing single or double flowers. A single fuchsia flower is defined as one which has four sepals and four petals. Unfortunately many plants which, when first produced, showed only four petals and were therefore described in catalogues as single have started to produce flowers with five or more petals. Such plants should be examined very carefully and any flowers not true to the description should be removed. At one stage any plants showing erring flowers were marked NAS, but nowadays the judges are asked to downpoint the plants concerned. A true double flower will have eight or more petals and there are classes within most schedules particularly for this type of plant. There is an intermediate category, semi-double, for flowers which have five, six or seven petals. It is very rare to find a show catering specifically for this type of flower and it has become common practice to exhibit this type of plant within the classes designated doubles.

Bushes and Shrubs

Type of growth is also an important factor. Most schedules call for plants that are bush or shrub trained. The ruling body of the British Fuchsia world, the British Fuchsia Society, have laid down certain definitions for the various types of training and most affiliated societies follow these rulings, their shows being judged according to British Fuchsia Society Standards.

To the layman there appears to be very little difference between a bush and a shrub, but closer examination will reveal that a bush is grown on a single stem coming from the compost. This stem must not exceed 1½ inches in length. A shrub on the other hand can have any number of growths coming from the compost. A plant which has a stem longer than the maximum laid down will be judged not according to schedule. Most society shows ask for bush *or* shrub trained, although it is possible to find some schedules which specify one or the other, so read your schedule carefully.

Standards

There will always be classes in the show for specialised types of growth. The most common of these is that of standards. Many members of the public think of these plants as tree fuchsias, and it is fair to say that this is a good description. Briefly, a standard fuchsia is a bush grown on a straight stem of varying length – methods of training plants have been described elsewhere.

Mini Standard

This must be grown in a pot not exceeding 5 inches (13 cm) in diameter and which has a clear stem (from soil level to the first break) of no more than ten inches. There is no minimum length laid down but for proportional reasons a length of 6–7 inches (15–18cm) would be most appropriate.

Quarter Standard

This has a clear stem of between 10 inches (25cm) and 18 inches (46cm) in length. It can usually be grown in any size of pot although the size may be stipulated in the schedule. The proportions of the head, the stem, and the pot are important factors to consider. The stem of the quarter standard can be supported with a stake and the plant neatly tied to it.

Half Standard

This standard has a clear stem of between 18 inches (46cm) and 30 inches (76cm), and can usually be exhibited in any size of pot. A stake support is permissible and ties should be neat and tidy. The size of the head should again be in proportion to the length of the stem – try to aim for a stem of two-thirds and a head of one-third.

Full Standard

This has a minimum clear stem length of 30 inches (76cm) and a maximum of 42 inches (107cm). Again any sized pot is permitted, and a stake can be used to support the rather heavy head. Again consideration should be given to the proportional sizes of the stem and the head.

Baskets

Other classes which will appear on all show schedules call for baskets, half baskets and hanging pots. These are excellent classes to look at and are usually well supported. It is always best to look up into the flowers, as in this way you can see the 'ballerina skirt' which attracts so many people. For the purposes of shows there is usually a maximum size laid down for the diameter of the basket. Generally this is 15 inches (38cm) but it can vary from show to show. Full baskets, if the show follows the British Fuchsia Society guidelines, should be hemi-spherical in shape, that is with a rounded base. There is no restriction on the make of the basket, wire or plastic are equally as acceptable. The half baskets, sometimes called wall baskets, are half a full basket – in other words semi-hemi-spherical. Again, flat-bottomed baskets are not acceptable.

The description of these classes usually states 'fuchsias only'; other types of plants sometimes found growing in hanging baskets are therefore not allowed. I would also add the suggestion here that the basket should contain just one variety of fuchsia and not a mixture. You may have as many plants as you wish in the basket, although five would be an adequate number for the maximum-sized container. The reason for not mixing the varieties is quite simply that differing types develop, mature and grow at differing rates. You should be aiming at even growth with flowers all around the basket, and using one type of fuchsia is by far the best method of achieving this result.

Hanging Pot

The hanging pot class is relatively new to the schedules, but it is gaining popularity. Examine the wording of the schedule carefully to determine whether one or more plants are permitted in each pot. The size of the pot might also be stipulated as also might be the type of pot. I would suggest that for the hanging pot, which is smaller than a basket, a small flowered cultivar will be the best to use.

Hardies

Very often there are classes specifically for plants considered to be hardy. When this word appears it is advisable again to look carefully at the schedule to see if the description follows the BFS hardy list, or whether the society has produced its own list of eligible plants.

Species

Classes for species or *Encliandra* group fuchsias appear in schedules – note the size of the pot permitted and also whether a list of eligible plants is included.

Any Sized Pots

Somewhere in the schedule there is usually a class for plants grown in any size of pot. In this class it is usually possible to display the large structures and specially shaped plants such as pillars, fans, pyramids and espalier. Again, though, ensure that these different types of training are permitted. These are always very eye catching specimens and are usually strong contenders for the award of best plant in the show.

Individual Flowers

Most popular with visitors and an easy class to start with in your show life is the class calling for six fuchsia flowers displayed upon a board (which is usually provided). It should be possible for anyone interested in fuchsias to gather six different blooms on the morning of the show and to arrange them tastefully. What you should be looking for is absolute perfection – there should be no faults in any of the flowers, they should be young and fresh and should be correctly named. It is possible here to show off those large flowers which have come from plants which are not themselves show specimens. The transportation of these perfect blooms so that no bruising occurs is no easy task, but there is great satisfaction in winning these hotly-contested classes.

Displays

Another opportunity to display plants which are themselves not individually perfect is in the class calling for a display of plants in a restricted area (usually a square of 2 feet 6 inches, or 76cm). Here is a chance to show some ingenuity in grouping together numerous plants to give a very pleasing overall picture. It is not advisable to leave the planning of this class until the last minute as some excellent results can be obtained by giving prior thought to the training of some of the plants.

I have not attempted to cover every possible type of class that will be met in show schedules – they do vary considerably in differing parts of the country – but I hope that I have whetted your appetite and that you will be prepared to have a go in the near future. There are pitfalls and mistakes which many beginners make to start with, but most of these can be avoided by reading the schedule very carefully, and asking for advice (even right up to the very end when plants are about to be placed on the show bench) from the show secretary, show stewards or any other exhibitors.

JUDGING FUCHSIAS

When visiting a show, purely as a spectator, you are able to witness the culmination of many months of dedicated work. Work by the growers in their efforts to produce plants which attract the public (after all the society show is the society shop window); work by the organisers in preparing a stage upon which the plants can be shown; work by the judges who meticulously examine each plant so that they can be placed in the correct order of merit. Each of these factors must be present or there would be no show.

The judge certainly has a very important and responsible part to play, as dissatisfaction with the judging will deter competitors from entering on future occasions. The task is not easy but it certainly can be very enjoyable. The most important item in a judge's armoury is a love and intimate knowledge of fuchsias and their methods of growing. A judge must be capable of growing fuchsias to exhibition standard – only with this qualification does he know what to look for in a good plant. An excellent exhibitor will make an excellent judge as each exhibitor has, of necessity, to judge his own plants prior to every show.

Before every show the judge should be provided with a copy of the show schedule – this should be done well in advance of the show so that there is time to study it very carefully. This will give the judge some idea of what to expect when arriving at the venue. Each judge will have his own particular way of approaching each class so it would be presumptuous of anyone to lay down guide-lines for all judges to follow – I can only speak for myself and the way in which I carry out this duty. Each class within a show is a separate entity and is judged as such. A walk along the benches, viewing all the plants within the class, will give a good idea of the overall standard. As you judge you will be accompanied by show stewards whose first task will have been to point out where the class started and where it ends. The number of plants within the class is useful information to have at hand. Most shows have two judges working together but the initial examination of the plants should be done individually. Having examined the plants generally it is usually possible to sort out those plants which are in with a chance and those which are not. Some will be manifestly better than others and stand out well. Examining the various classes in more detail will help to illustrate what the judges are looking for.

Bushes and Shrubs

The size of the plant will depend greatly upon the size of the pot in which it is shown. If the class calls for plants in 3½ inch (9cm) pots, then the size of the plant should be proportional to that. Biggest is not always best – it is possible to grow very large plants in this size of pot by root pruning through the season, but very large plants in 3½ inch (9cm) pots look, and are wrong. Plants growing in 3½inch (9cm) pots should be very fresh looking and young – they should, in my opinion, be grown from cuttings taken during the current season. The flowers should be typical of the cultivar and should be, if possible, the first flush of flowers. The amount of flowers will vary a lot from cultivar to cultivar – a small flowered single would be expected to have many more flowers than a large flowered double. If the class has called for single flowers, then every flower on the plant should conform to that definition, with four sepals and four petals. Any flowers which do not conform should be noted and the plant downgraded. The exhibitor should have removed as many of these erring flowers as possible before the show. Great care should have been taken to remove any flowers which are past their best, and seed pods removed.

The foliage should be clean and fresh and should completely cover the whole of the plant. The plant should give the impression of symmetry and be presentable from any direction. There should be no sign of any pests or diseases and any supporting stakes used (although with this sized plant none should be necessary) should be as inconspicuous as possible. Any ties used should be neat and tidy. The plant should be labelled with its correct name and the pot should be clean.

There should be no debris in the top of the pot and the whole impression should be one of cleanliness and health.

Plants shown in classes asking for a maximum pot size of 5 inches (13cm) should be proportionally larger. These will probably be plants grown from late autumn cuttings or on the biennial method. There will therefore be a greater number of branches and greater depth in the head. The number of flowers will depend upon the cultivar exhibited but a very good coverage of flowers is expected. Supports are more likely with plants that have been grown from spring cuttings as the growth will be more open and lax. Such supports should be as inconspicuous as possible and any ties unobtrusive.

Where two different types of growth are possible, a certain amount of subjectivity will be necessary. Some judges like an open, natural type of growth whilst others admire the closely-knit plants that are produced by continuously pinching over a long season. For this reason it is advisable to have more than one judge making the decisions. Again, though, it is important that the plant should be symmetrical and look well-balanced from every direction. The judges are likely to remove the plants from the benches and look at them from above, as this will give them an idea of the overall roundness and also whether there is any hollowing in the centre. Cleanness of foliage, flowers and pots will also be taken into consideration.

The comments made with regard to plants in 5 inch (13cm) pots apply equally to plants shown in 6 inch (15cm) pots. Larger sized plants will be expected, having enjoyed greater root space during their growing period. These general comments apply to all classes calling for bush or shrub trained plants and apply even to those specialised classes, such as for plants of the *triphylla* type, or those on the hardy list. Judging the plants in species classes calls for slightly different appraisal, and is discussed later.

Standards

Again it does not necessarily follow that biggest is best. The head of the plant should be proportional to the length of the stem, with roughly two thirds for the stem one third for the head. The width of the head also needs to be roughly in proportion. The stem of the plant is a most important factor, as its length will decide whether the plant qualifies for quarter, half or full standard. These measurements need to be taken very carefully, measuring from the surface of the compost in the pot to the first break, which can be a leaf or a branch coming from the main stem. Would-be exhibitors need to be aware of these measurements, especially where their plants are very close to one of the dividing lines. Additional compost in the pot will reduce the length of stem and, conversely, compost removed from the pot will lengthen it. It is strongly advised though that these measurements should be taken into consideration when the plant is in the growing stage.

The stem should be as straight as possible and should be free from blemishes. The plant may be supported by a stake (a single stake only), and the stem attached to this stake with strong but neat ties. The head needs to be as round as possible and should be a mass of good clean foliage with abundant flowers. No dead or dying flowers or foliage should be present and the flowers should be typical of the cultivar being shown. Seed pods should not be present. The required measurements for standards are given in the previous section.

Full Baskets

The judge will expect the basket to conform to the descriptions laid down in the schedule. The diameter of the basket will have been specified as will its shape. Some societies permit baskets with flat bottoms, others do not. Some insist that the baskets must be round whilst others will accept a hanging container, that is wooden slatted baskets. These regulations in the schedule must be adhered to.

Baskets are generally exhibited by either hanging them from an overhead bar or by placing them on a stand on the show bench. It is important for the judge to be able to look into the basket to examine it for any debris that might have accumulated during the growing season. It is not unknown for birds nests to have been found in well grown baskets. The foliage of the plants in a basket is usually very thick so examination is sometimes a little difficult. The judge will expect to see a basket completely covered with foliage and flowers, in fact it should not be possible to see the actual basket from any direction when viewed at eye level.

The foliage and the flowers should sweep, or cascade over the edge and continue until at least the depth of the basket. There should be flowers covering the whole of the basket and not just at the ends of the laterals. The centre of the basket should be of a good height, and the overall impression should be of a great ball of flowers. The judge will still be on the look-out for dead and dying flowers or foliage and any seed pods which have escaped the attention of the exhibitor. There can be any number of plants in the basket although it is advisable to use plants of only one cultivar in each basket. This is not mandatory but it would be difficult to get the evenness of growth necessary to make a good basket if different cultivars were used.

Half Baskets (Wall Baskets)

These are normally displayed against a wall, and the same criteria for judging the full baskets applies with half baskets. The shape will have been determined by the schedule. The judge will look at the basket at eye level and will also look at it from the front and the sides. If possible, foliage and flowers should start from the wall on one side of the basket and then sweep round to the other side. No part of the actual basket should be visible to the viewer.

Hanging Pots

Again the definition in the schedule is important as there are a number of different types of hanging pot available. Usually the schedule will ask for a single plant in the pot, so the judges will be on the look-out for any exhibits showing multiple plants. The same criteria as for baskets will apply when judging hanging pots, and the pot should be completely covered with foliage and flowers. They will be judged at eye level. My personal preference is that the plants grown in these pots should be of the smaller flowering types, but there is no real reason why larger flowered varieties should not be used.

Species

The classes for species are not usually very well supported, although it is possible at some shows to come across some very good examples. The most important point with regard to the showing of species is that they should be grown with a minimum of training. Usually one stop at the beginning of the season will suffice to get a good bushy plant. It is important to have good clean foliage right down to the level of the pot; a major fault with many plants is that they show bare stems. The flowers should be as plentiful as possible, bearing in mind the type of species being shown. It is often very difficult, as there is usually only one class for species, for the judges to compare a very large growing variety with a short creeping type. When showing this type of plant it is not necessary to remove the seed pods as this is part of their attraction. Occasionally the schedule will stipulate that the plant can be shown in any size of pot, but at other times a 6 inch (15cm) maximum is asked for.

The plants of the Encliandra group are normally shown separately. The flowers and leaves of these plants are extremely small but some excellent plants can be grown with a minimum of training. Cleanness of foliage and an abundance of small flowers will be expected.

Large Structures

Occasionally in a schedule a class can be found asking for plants of a specific type of training such as pillars, pyramids, fans or espaliers. If such a class is not included, you will often find that this type of training is permitted in a class for plants grown in any size of pot. Plants thus displayed are always a great attraction and the size, plus the difficulty of growing and transporting, often lead to best in the show. But it should not be taken as a foregone conclusion, as even these large specimens need to be well grown and well presented. They need to have good foliage and flowers covering the whole of the structure. They too should be clean of spent foliage, dead flowers and seed pods. It is more difficult to keep such structures free from pests and diseases but this is nevertheless essential.

Small Pot Culture

It is possible in most schedules to have a class for plants grown under the rules for small pot culture. These rules are very simple in that the maximum size of pot permitted is 5 inches (13cm), and the maximum height of the foliage from compost to the apex for pyramids, pillars, fans or espaliers is 20 inches (50cm). The maximum length of clear stem for miniature standards is 10 inches (25cm).

This is an excellent class to aim for if you want to grow something different. Unfortunately most exhibitors concentrate on the mini standards and very few of the other types are seen. With all of these structures it is possible to get a good plant in one season from a very early cutting so the judges will expect to see fresh young-looking foliage and an abundance of good flowers typical of the cultivar being grown. I suggest that, as you are growing plants in miniature, small flowered cultivars would be the better ones to choose. Mini baskets may also be entered in this class. The maximum size for these is a diameter of 6 inches (15cm). In all other respects the judging will be the same as for a full basket.

Displays

One of the nicest classes in a show is the display, usually in a small area of about 2 feet 6 inches square (76cm). In this class it is possible to exhibit those plants which have not quite made the grade as individuals; plants which are one-sided because of lack of attention to the daily turning can be used. The judging of this type of class is bound to be subjective so it is important to have as eye-catching a display as possible. Unusual training methods for certain plants can be used to get a shape you desire. The plants should be well presented and should be clean and free of pests, diseases and all the other faults previously mentioned.

Individual Blooms

This is the class which attracts most attention and which is usually the judges' nightmare. Six blooms are usually asked for and the mounting to be used is generally provided by the show organisers. The flowers should be perfect in all respects. There should be no blemishes at all and the freshness can be displayed by having fresh pollen on the stamens. It is recommended that, if six flowers are called for, they should be a good mixture of colour and form. If no specification is made on the schedule that they should all be different it is possible to enter two or even three of the same cultivars. The judge will be looking for faults, but well presented flowers with contrasting singles and doubles and contrasting colours are likely to win the day.

Major Awards

In most shows it is the task of the judge to award a special prize to the plant or group which is considered to be the best in the show. This is not an easy task as it is necessary to compare plants which are of differing sizes. The winning plants of all the classes will be considered for this honour, although it is possible that a single plant from a group which in its entirety did not receive a ticket will be considered. The only way in which these plants can be compared with each other is by placing the individual plants close together. They can then be judged as though they were an individual class. This is a difficult task but a most important one, as the final decision carries the ultimate award for which every grower strives.

These are some of the points that the judges will be looking for as they examine your plants. I hope that I have not dissuaded you from entering the showing arena. It can be very good fun and the camaraderie that one meets before, during and after the show reflects the friendliness of those who grow the fuchsia.

SHOW DAY

Transporting and Dressing

Show day is the culmination of the work of a long season. For many that season will have started some fifteen months earlier – it is a great pity, then, if all this work is wasted by lack of care at the last stage. If the object has been to produce plants for the show bench then it is absolutely essential that a specimen as perfect as possible should be presented.

The very first decision to be made is what plants to enter, and in what classes on the schedule. It is therefore important to obtain a copy of the Show Schedule at the earliest possible opportunity. These are usually obtainable from about March onwards and the show organiser will be able to supply you with one. If you have entered the show previously then it is very likely that you will receive one without having to ask. Read the schedule very carefully and decide at an early stage which classes you will be entering. Please don't be tempted to send in your entry forms too soon – there is nothing more frustrating for a show organiser than to arrange space for an exhibit on the show bench and for it to fail to turn up. It is far better to leave your entry until you are absolutely certain what you will have available. If by any chance you are unable to fulfil your entry commitments, please contact the show organiser so that the space can be used for some other purpose.

Having made your decision it is now possible to estimate the number of plants that you will need to carry to the show. If you have been growing large specimens then special arrangements will probably have to be made. If you have friends in the vicinity who will also be displaying at the same show it might be possible to come to some arrangement regarding the hire of large transport. It is a good idea in the first instance to try to work out what the problems are actually likely to be, and having decided that, you will be part of the way towards finding a solution. The object is to get plants to the show in first class condition. The foliage and flowers need to be intact and unbruised, all the branches need to be complete. Baskets must have unbruised foliage and flowers and the trailing branches undamaged. Similarly, the heads of standards need to be kept intact with no bruising to the leaves or flowers.

Bouncing up and down or shaking backwards and forwards in a car or van is likely to cause damage to foliage and bloom and possibly even to branches, so some means of keeping these as static as possible must be devised. They will probably have to be packed fairly close together but that could cause bruising to the foliage and flowers. No matter how carefully you may drive there is always the chance that another driver or a pedestrian will do something silly and cause you to brake violently.

Solving the first problem is easy – you can keep the plants from falling over by providing them with a heavy base into which the pot will fit. It does not require a great deal of imagination to devise some such method, whether it is a much larger and heavier pot, nails sticking up out of blocks of wood, blocks of concrete, or concrete blocks which have a moulded pot shape built in, to hold them upright. All these methods will keep the pots still and prevent them from toppling. But they will not stop the foliage and flowers from brushing against each other with the movement of the car, so some other method must be devised to prevent damage.

One such method is to cover the whole of the head of the plant with a soft muslin cover. Muslin sleeves are available at most garages and are generally used for polishing the car. They are not expensive to buy and come in quite economical lengths. I describe them as sleeves because they consist of a long soft muslin tube. These have the flexibility to expand sideways and will therefore hold the upper foliage of a plant very still when placed in position.

The task of wrapping up the plants for the show is an acquired art and one that needs to be practised well in advance of the show. It is essential to get assistance with this delicate task. Your partner puts his arms through the centre of a length of sleeve (approximately 3 feet long would be a reasonable length for a plant growing in a 6 inch pot). Your helper will then hold the pot, upside down with fingers over the compost preventing the plant from falling out. In this position all the foliage and flowers will be hanging down towards the ground. Very gently the muslin sleeve is then eased down over the pot and over the complete plant – this sounds drastic but it is in fact quite easy. When the plant is completely covered by the muslin it can be returned to an upright position. The muslin can be pulled up a little higher and then tied above the foliage. The plant is now ready for transportation and there will be no movement of foliage or flowers which would have caused the bruising. Another advantage is that plants prepared in this way will take up far less space in the back of any vehicle.

On arrival at the show ground it will be possible to reverse the process. Again two people are required for preference although it is possible for one to carry out the task quite successfully. The plant should be stood in an upright position and the muslin cloth gently pulled up over it. When completely free, the branches of the plant will fall back into place and it will look as good, if not better, than it did at home.

This method of covering can also be used for the standards although the head of a very large standard will take some covering. Under these circumstances a variation of the idea with wide strips of muslin being used to hold the branches and foliage in position would be sensible.

The transportation of large baskets can cause quite a bit of difficulty. One of the safest methods would be to use a shorter version of the type of basket stand used on the show benches. Provided the base of any such structure used to support the basket is much wider than the top, stability should be assured. Half baskets, if more than one are being transported, can be carried in the same way with two being placed back to back. Very large structures will give problems but once the problem has been diagnosed the solution will probably follow. Stability of base and lack of movement in the foliage and flowers is the objective.

Having arrived at the show ground you must now set about staging the plants. Rule number one, is to allow yourself plenty of time. Unload your plants and place them in a convenient position, still wrapped up, close to the show benches. Most show organisers arrange for there to be 'dressing' tables available and these should be used. Do not unpack your plants straight on to the show benches. Obtain your entry cards from the show organiser and, if there are any gaps in your entry, inform him at this time. Look around the benches to find out exactly where your plants will need to be placed, and find out, if you can, how many other exhibits there will be in each of the classes you are entering.

You will already know, having decided before leaving home, exactly what plants are to be exhibited and in which classes. An extra label or some means of identification on each pot is valuable. Try to go through your classes in numerical order, removing each plant, as required, from its covering. You will probably find that there is little or no damage and that very little preparation of the plants will be necessary. Look each plant over very carefully, removing any dead or damaged foliage and flowers. Any seed pods which you have missed should also be removed. Make sure that all the flowers are standing out from the foliage and are not hiding away. Try not to touch the individual flowers but ease them out using a pencil or some such implement. Decide which is the most attractive side of the plant, although hopefully it will look equally good from all angles, and place it on the show bench in its correct position. Bearing in mind the number of other exhibits there will be, try not to be too greedy for space. Stand each plant in a saucer of the correct size for the pot. If the show is for more than one day then the organiser will see to the watering of the plants. If no saucers are in position under the pots then the water will seep through, and there is nothing more upsetting than to see a bench covered with water puddles. When you are satisfied that your plant is looking perfect, place the class card in front of it (with your name face downwards), ensure that a card bearing the name of the cultivar is in position in front of the pot, and leave it.

Proceed to the next class and continue the staging. If you are showing plants in a multi-pot class try to make them as attractive as you possibly can. With a three pot class it is advisable to have either two in front and one behind or the reverse. Your plants should be as equal in size as possible, but if they are not then the one that is larger or smaller can be placed on an upturned pot. This will not fool the judge into thinking they are all of the same size but it will give a better impression. A tall plant standing on a pot at the back of a trio only looks taller because it is standing on a pot. The choice of plants for a multiple class will have been made before leaving home but an attempt should always be made to match colours and form.

Proceed through all the classes, checking with your schedule all the time that you are placing the plants in the right position and that they fit the description defined in the schedule for each class. If a class asks for five distinct cultivars then ensure that they are distinctive. If a class calls for single flowering cultivars then make sure that each flower on your plant has only four petals. If the class calls for cultivars do not include any plants of the species. Make sure that you are displaying plants grown in the correct sizes of pots – most plastic pots have the size imprinted on the base of the pot so there should really be no mistake. If you are using good old-fashioned clay pots then it will be necessary to measure them carefully. The diameter at the top of the pot should roughly equal the height of the pot. Do not worry if you do not know the name of the cultivar – place a small card in front of your exhibit asking the Judge to name. Plants are not downgraded if they are not named although it might be taken into consideration in a very close competition.

Make sure that you have a supply of spare pots, saucers and canes with you, as accidents do happen. Some spare plants might also come in very useful. If you have failed to do so before, place your plant in a clean pot of the same size – dirty pots detract from the overall appearance of the plant. Check over your baskets very carefully, getting right inside the foliage and removing any debris that may have accumulated. This should have been done before you left home but a final clean up is always a good idea.

If you are in any doubt about any aspect of the show please ask. You will always find that everyone is anxious to help you, officials, fellow competitors and any others who might be around. Above all, enjoy yourself – fuchsia shows are not cut-throat affairs, there is always a great feeling of friendship, and constructive advice is always available. If you are entering for the very first time do not worry – any help you need will be willingly given.

Take your time over the staging but make sure that you do have time for a final look over your plants before the end of the time allocated for staging. Once you are satisfied that your plants are presented to your satisfaction then leave the arena, clearing away any debris that you may have made in your preparations, and relax. There is nothing more that you can do until the judges have completed their deliberations.

When the show is officially open to the public you may return to the benches to see how successful you have been. If you are disappointed with the results, try to find out why your plants were not considered for higher positions. It may be obvious when you compare yours with the winning exhibits, but if it is not do not be afraid to ask. The judges are usually in attendance for most of the time the show is open and will welcome the opportunity to explain their reasoning. If you are satisfied with the result and you have good reason to be proud of your achievements then, with magnanimity, remain in the immediate vicinity of your best plants and bathe in their reflected glory. There is no greater fillip to one's ego than to hear the comment, 'How on earth did they manage to grow a plant as good as that?' Little will they realise that the plants grew themselves and that you only helped – just a little.

Finally, if you have been successful in winning trophies, make sure that you know when the presentation will be taking place. If you have prize money to collect make sure you do so before the end of the show. When given permission to clear the benches (this time is usually stated in the schedule), do so quickly, packing them away as carefully as you did when you brought them.

BIENNIAL GROWING FOR SHOWING

Without doubt the biggest and best plants on the show bench are those growing in 6 inch pots, which have taken almost two years to reach maturity. Two years seems a very long time, especially as it is possible to produce a very reasonable sized plant in about six months.

The object of the biennial system of growing is so that a good plant can be built up in one year, and flower for the first time the next year. In fairness, though, it must be said that this is not a method that is to be recommended unless you have sufficient space and are able to maintain a fairly high temperature throughout the winter months. You will need to maintain a temperature in the region of 45 degrees Fahrenheit (7°C) so that the plants will not go into a dormant state but will continue growing steadily. Some growers might say they have achieved quite good results even though the greenhouse temperature has only been kept just higher than freezing point. This may well be so, but a higher temperature is certainly beneficial to the plants. The object is really to keep the plants just ticking over, not actually growing, as with the light intensity so low in the darker months of the year any growth that is made will be thin and spindly.

The end of April and the beginning of May are the ideal times to take your cuttings. At that time of the year there will be ample supplies of cutting material so it will be possible to choose the strongest and firmest pieces. As there is no shortage it is wise to take more cuttings than you need, and you may then select the strongest growing plants once they have rooted. In any batch of cuttings there are those which seem to get away the fastest and will build up into the strongest plants. Use those and dispose of the remainder.

The best type of cuttings are the smallest of small tip cuttings. These are often referred to as ultra green tip cuttings. A considerable number of these very small cuttings can be inserted in a small area so the process can be very economical. The compost should be one which contains a certain amount of nutrient, and I suggest that a mixture of 50 per cent ordinary compost of the type you usually use, with 50 per cent perlite or vermiculite. My preference would be for vermiculite as it is softer. By adding either of these two products you are diluting the nutrient factor of the compost, assisting its drainage qualities and yet also increasing its moisture holding capabilities.

Some advance thinking needs to go into the preparation of the plants which will be providing the cuttings. It is always important to take cuttings from good strong healthy plants which have been well watered the day before so that the branches and shoots will be fully charged with moisture. The plants should have been well sprayed with a combined insecticide and fungicide during the week prior to taking the cuttings. It might also be an added insurance against botrytis if the compost is well moistened with a good systemic fungicide (such as Nimrod T) prior to the insertion of the cuttings.

The smallest of tip cuttings only will be used and should be gently pushed into the compost so that the next pair of leaves is just resting on the compost. Above this pair of leaves there will be just one more pair and the small growing tip. Once they have been inserted into the compost, and labelled, they should be given a very light watering using a very fine-rosed watering can so that the compost is settled around the cuttings. The firming of the compost in any way other than by using the watering can is not recommended.

When all of the cuttings have been taken the trays or pots should be placed in a propagator, not necessarily to provide warmth as the outside temperature is probably sufficient to help rooting, but to provide the humid atmosphere around the cuttings which will prevent too much loss of moisture through transpiration. If the thermostat of the propagator is set at 65 degrees Fahrenheit (18°C) that will be ideal should the outside temperature fall. One of the major enemies to rooting now is dryness. It is therefore necessary to prevent rays from the hot sun from shining through the glass of the greenhouse and the propagator on to the unrooted cuttings. Even a few minutes in that type of dry heat will be sufficient to ruin a complete batch of cuttings. A sheet of paper over the propagator will suffice and if this is in addition to the shading of the greenhouse there should be no great difficulty.

The cuttings must be kept turgid so a regular inspection and spraying with tepid water is advisable, to prevent them from wilting. Many growers prefer not to place these cuttings under the cover of a propagator but to have them open – this will mean that there is a greater risk of loss of moisture by transpiration as the cuttings will not be contained in a humid atmosphere. Cuttings which are left open will need regular spraying, perhaps two or three times daily, or the services of an automatic mist spray. The argument that leaving the cuttings in the open prevents the possibility of the young cuttings being drawn towards the light as soon as they have formed their roots and started to grow is a valid one. However, regular inspection and an awareness that rooting has taken place will alleviate this problem even if the cuttings were covered throughout their rooting process.

As soon as a reasonable root ball has been formed at the base of the cutting – and the appearance of the cuttings, with a gloss on the leaves, will soon inform you of this stage – the young plants should be potted on to their first individual pots. Now is the time to make your first decision as to which plants are to be retained and which given away. If the cuttings were rooted in a pot containing a number of cuttings then they should be separated. Little damage is done, in fact it is probably beneficial, if all the old compost is washed away from the roots. If the cuttings have been rooted in individual cells of a tray, this process need not be followed, but the plants potted on directly into their new pots and compost. The compost used on this occasion should be the full strength compost that you usually use, but make sure that it is a compost which contains a good proportion of drainage material as the plants must be able to breathe through their roots. Once they have been transferred to their new pots they should be given preferential treatment for a couple of days, keeping them shaded from the sun and spraying overhead so that they will not suffer any great set back from their traumatic move.

The training of these plants should start as soon as they have become established in their pots. If the plants are required for bush or shrub plants then the growing tips should be removed as soon as two or three pairs of leaves have been formed. Only the very smallest part of the tip should be removed, taking care not to damage the embryonic shoots that there will be in the top pair of leaf axils. If the plants are required as standards then it will not be necessary to remove the growing tip, but the plants should be encouraged to grow straight and firm. This process of pinching out the growing tips will continue throughout the season as soon as each shoot has developed two pairs of leaves and the growing tip. The object is to build up a dense pattern of branches at a very early stage which will be the foundation for superb plants later. The plants will look small and appear to have stopped growing, but you can check the progress of the training simply by counting the number of shoots.

From the beginning of June onwards, every opportunity should be taken to grow these plants out of doors, so that they grow hard. At this time they will be in their first pots, that is 3 inch (7½cm) pots; do not be in any hurry to move these plants on into larger pots, as the aim is to reach a maximum of 5 inch (13cm) pots by the end of the year. One of the problems will be that the pot will soon become full of roots, making the plant feel threatened so that it starts to produce flowers. The plant will not feel threatened if root movement continues or if feeding takes place, so a regular pattern of feeding is vital – at the start of the season, use a high nitrogen content feed. It will not hurt the plant either if, once the pot has become full of roots, it is removed and some of the older compost teased away. The new compost replacing the old will encourage the plant to keep growing.

It might well be advisable to have a special structure into which these plants can be placed, as they require a vibrant atmosphere, with plenty of air going around and through the leaves. The very nature of the training, building up a close network of branches, will mean that the risk of botrytis in the centre of the plant will always be present unless such air movement is present – stagnant conditions encourage such diseases. Many growers build a special structure covered with a fairly fine netting. This has considerable advantages in that even in gale force winds the plants will be receiving a gentle breeze and in the event of a heavy thunder storm the droplets will be broken down into a gentle misty rain. With the additional advantage of shading from the direct rays of the sun that such structures provide, ideal growing conditions should be created.

The base of the structure can be covered with a sheet of polythene upon which a layer of gravel chippings can be placed. Each time the plants are watered, and this must be done regularly and carefully throughout the growing season, the gravel will become moistened and a cool moist atmosphere around the plants will be maintained. The importance of having a well-drained compost will now be obvious, as the plants receive a lot of water during the growing season. Keep feeding them with a high nitrogen feed – it is often suggested that a very dilute feed at every watering is better than a feast once a day or once a week.

As the season progresses it is very likely that the plants will want to flower but they should not be allowed to do so. Remove any flower buds as soon as they can be easily handled. If they persist then it might be necessary to remove the plants from their pots, remove some of the compost and repot using a small amount of fresh compost. By the end of August the plants will be bursting to get out of the 3 inch (7½cm) pots and can be moved on into 4 inch (10cm) pots.

Towards the end of September you should seriously consider bringing the plants back into the greenhouse, as it is not unknown to have frosts early in October. Before doing so it is important to ensure that the environment into which we will be bringing the plants is ideal for them. The greenhouse should be scrupulously cleaned, removing everything from it before giving the inside a thorough clean with disinfectant.

Carefully check all your heating equipment. If you are using paraffin heaters make sure that they are clean and that the wick is still in good condition, replacing it if necessary. Make sure that you have adequate supplies of fuel, or that there is no possibility of running out at a crucial time. If you are heating by gas check that your heaters are working well and that the thermostats are satisfactory. Electricity is perhaps the easiest and cleanest to use, but again check that all the equipment is satisfactory.

Bear in mind that heating the whole of a large greenhouse would be an expensive exercise; and also bear in mind that when all your biennial plants are brought into the greenhouse they should not be occupying any more than half of the total area. This being so it would be rather foolhardy to heat the whole of the greenhouse with half of it empty, so arrangements could be made to partition off half of the area using a permanent structure or a curtain of polythene. Also check on your ventilation system – during the winter we often get some clear days when the sun shines through the glass so good ventilation will be imperative. Also remember that we have spent a long time building up a plant structure which is very thick and heavy with branches so an air current through these plants is vital.

Once the house is ready, make a careful check of your plants. They have been growing well, have filled their 4 inch (10cm) pots with roots and become covered with a good layer of leaves. The occasional flower bud is probably still appearing and must be removed before it develops too much. Hidden within this foliage it is possible that there will be a number of uninvited guests – green fly, white fly, and red spider mites. You must be positive that all such pests have been destroyed before bringing them into the greenhouse and providing them with the type of atmosphere which will encourage them to multiply freely. Each plant should be examined carefully and given a very thorough spraying with a combined insecticide and fungicide; alternatively, the whole plant, pot and all, can be dipped into a good solution of this combined treatment so that all pests, seen and unseen, are removed.

October and November are not easy months. The temperature during the day might well encourage the plants to grow but the lower light intensity will only encourage thin, long jointed growth – the very thing we have been trying to avoid. The air both inside and outside the house is likely to be charged with moisture and most conducive to botrytis, so keep the air moving as much as possible by using a fan, or by having the vents and doors open at all times when frost is not threatened.

Towards the end of December you may be a little worried by plants which are beginning to look decidedly unhealthy;

you do not wish to increase the heat yet and spraying only serves to increase the moisture content of the greenhouse. The lower leaves on the plants may have been dropping and, although they are being replaced with smaller leaves, you may be anxious that only bare stemmed plants will remain for next season. There is no need to worry, however, as brighter weather and longer days with a higher light intensity approach, when all will be remedied. Even so, you may still help your plants by removing them from their pots, on a bright sunny wintry day, to remove some of the old compost and repot them into 5 inch (13cm) pots. This will encourage them to form new roots, but fast growth is prevented by keeping the temperature down.

As winter turns to spring, the plants will take on a far more robust look. In fact they will be looking as though they are ready to burst out of their pots. Potting on into 6 inch (15cm) pots should be carried out in the early days of March, again first removing some of the spent compost and replacing with new. At this repotting you should see a pot full of lovely fresh white roots, not the old brown gnarled type normally seen when repotting old plants at this time of the year. The temperature in the greenhouse will be rising along with the outside temperature, but this may need to be supplemented at night by raising the thermostat so that a minimum of 55 degrees Fahrenheit (12°C) is maintained. As the light intensity increases, the plants will grow rapidly into super specimens.

Keep pinching out the growing tips of the new shoots as soon as two pairs of leaves have been formed, but bear in mind that as the date for the show approaches it will be necessary to discontinue this pinching out at the appropriate time, a time which will vary according to a number of factors.

Two main things must be taken into consideration. The first is the type of flower that the plant will produce – will it be a single or a double flower? A single flower needs less time to reach maturity than the double, in fact you will need to leave a period of eight to ten weeks for singles and ten to twelve weeks for doubles. Taking singles as an example, after a period of about six weeks the new shoots will have reached the same stage of development as the shoot which was pinched out. So, if there were small flower buds in the tips of your shoots at that time, after a period of six weeks there will once again be very small flower buds on the new shoots. With the doubles a period of eight weeks is required for this development. A further two weeks must then be allowed for the flower buds to develop into full-blown blooms. It is not possible to be any more exact with lengths of time required, as there are many variables – the cultivar chosen, the temperature, and the light intensity are all matters which need to be taken into consideration.

Another important factor though is to ensure that the shoots you need to pinch out are at the right stage of development to be able to do so. This really means that you will have to look back even further into a gardening calendar to decide when not the last stopping but the penultimate one should be. If you accept the rule of thumb that the shoots will develop sufficiently between stops in a period of three weeks, then that penultimate stop must be made eleven weeks prior to the show for singles and thirteen weeks before the show for doubles. If you find that the plants are ready before the time set for the penultimate stop, delay the operation until the suggested date, as it is easier to remove a slightly larger piece of tip than to remove a piece that is not correctly formed. If the final two stops are carried out at the suggested time, you should have flowers on your plants for show days. It is also a good idea to record the dates of your final stoppings as you do them, and then note when the first flowers appear. This information will be invaluable for future years so that your actions will be more scientific and less hit-or-miss.

Throughout this period of rapid growth, from March through until flowering time, keep your plant well fed. A starved plant will try to flower early and the foliage will be small and privet-like. During the early part of the season feed with a high nitrogen feed, such as Chempak No. 2 or Vitafeed 3–0–1. As the season progresses, say in about June, change to a balanced food such as Chempak No. 3. You may also decide to use Phostrogen at this stage – I have not suggested using it earlier as, in spite of its excellence as a plant food, it does contain a higher percentage of potash. This may be invaluable for the ripening of wood and the density of flower colour, but it is less helpful in the growth of new wood. Once you have completed your stopping programme, it is advisable to change to a food with a high potash content. Phostrogen, Chempak No.4 or Vitafeed 1–0–3 would be ideal.

Two or three weeks prior to the show date, try to ensure that the blooms on display will be perfect and unmarked. Do not therefore trust them to the vagaries of the weather, rather take them inside the greenhouse where they can be given a little extra treatment. To ensure that the plants are free of pests for show day, use insecticide pins. It might also be advantageous to water in a systemic insecticide but under no circumstances attempt to use liquid sprays overhead as the buds and flowers will be severely marked.

Plants grown by this method are usually very strong in the stems and will require very little staking. If, however, after the final stopping the resultant shoots become a little long, it might be necessary to give some support. But any staking that you use should be as inconspicuous as possible.

Having taken this amount of time and trouble to get your plants to the size and peak of perfection necessary to win on the show bench, please do not 'spoil the ship for a ha'p'orth of tar'. Spend that little extra time when staging your plants to ensure that they look their best and that all of the flowers are looking outwards from the plant and are not hidden under the foliage.

LARGE STRUCTURES

Without doubt the type of plant which causes members of societies or members of the general public to stand back in amazement is the very large structure sometimes seen at national shows. Their admiration is shared equally between the plants themselves and those capable of growing such specimens. However, if you look at some of the very old books where fuchsias are described, you will see pictures of proud growers standing beside specimens which have reached six feet or more in height – plants of that type seemed to be the norm rather than the exception. There are probably many very valid reasons why our forebears were able to grow such plants and why it is neither practicable nor desirable to do so today, although there are always those who are prepared to sacrifice their time and effort to show that it is still possible. The growers of past years were, for the most part, gardeners of large estates, with plenty of time at their disposal and no anxieties regarding the supplying of heat or the necessary fertilisers. Today's growers are dedicated enthusiasts anxious to show that it is still possible to grow plants of equal merit, and I am grateful to one such grower, Adrian Cooper of Worcester, for permission to reproduce some of the methods he used in his quest for the perfect large-structured plant.

The general classification large structure can include such

methods of training as standards, full baskets, half baskets, fans, espaliers, pillars, and pyramids. The method of growth for each of these structures will be covered in some detail, but perhaps, before starting, a 'health warning' might be in order. It is fair to say that once embarking upon a growing programme such as this there will be little time to consider much else; these plants are likely to take over your whole life, needing special arrangements when holidays are being considered, and demanding many hours of careful, dedicated work. But, having achieved the necessary height and perfection of growth, you will have the satisfaction of knowing that it will remain one of your family for as many as eight to ten years. In the years following the initial growing stage, great care will be needed over the winter, and a great faith that those new young shoots will once again emerge in the spring. You must also supply sufficient space for their growth and storage.

Considerable care and thought needs to go into the choice of cultivar to use for a large structure. Well-tried hardy types might be the best to use, but strength and vigour are the major attributes that your plants need to have. Make sure that you start with excellent young plants. If you can buy in fresh stock for this purpose then please do – but choose your plants carefully, visiting the nursery of your choice to select the strongest of the cultivars you need. Purchase at least two of each sort. On return to your own greenhouse take cuttings from your purchases and root these – it might be possible to get two or more excellent cuttings from each. From the resultant young plants choose those which appear the strongest. These new plants will now be growing under your conditions in the compost of your choice and should therefore feel well and truly at home from the start.

In order to maintain good strong upward growth, you must ensure that there is a good, strong, *growing,* root system. If growth of roots stops then growth of the upper branches also stops. Removing the tips of the shoots always stimulates the growth and the subsequent growth is vigorous. Similarly if roots are pruned in the same way, the growth of the new roots will be vigorous. Hence, if you look after the roots the top will look after itself.

The method of root pruning used by Adrian Cooper in his admirable little book *Big is Beautiful,* is to plant out the young rooted cuttings into a standard seed tray so that there are twelve cuttings to each tray. Pinching out the tips of these young plants will be carried out according to the suggestions mentioned later, for each type of structure. When each has been pinched out for the third time the compost in the tray is allowed to almost dry out. The plants are then removed from the tray and all the compost is removed. from the root systems, first by shaking and then by agitating them in water. The roots are then dipped into a container of perlite. The roots now have a fair resemblance to an old man's beard, but all but about 2½ inches (6cm) of this root system will be cut off. The individual plants are then repotted into fresh compost – the perlite will assist in the moistening of the area around the roots and at the same time help to drain the compost in that area. The roots will therefore be in the ideal situation to grow well and quickly. The plants are placed in 3 inch (7½cm) pots, so that their training can commence. Never at any stage in the training should the pots become so full of roots that the plants feel starved, so it is important to be always ready to pot on into the next size of pot.

Over-wintering

These plants must be kept frost free. Cut back to ripe wood after the watering has been greatly reduced and the feeding has stopped. Then very slowly increase the water until young growth shows on the branches. Control the growth by the watering – if the plant continues to grow, reduce the water, but if it seems to be returning to rest increase the watering.

If you wish, the plant may be left completely dormant and new growth restarted in the spring, by spraying the plant each morning with tepid water. If you find that growth at the bottom of the structure is hard to restart then you will probably find success by lying the plant on its side. Do not change the compost until you want strong spring growth and check throughout the winter for signs of vine weevil larvae in the root ball. When removing the old compost, remove as much as you can and root prune at the same time. The old thick roots are of little use and by cutting these out you will be encouraging the young white feeder roots.

One word of warning, don't – in spite of the temptations – use the young growths of these structures as 'cutting' material. The growing tip that you remove when 'stopping' your plants should be only the smallest of small pieces, not really suitable for cutting material. Always give your plants as much air as possible, taking them out of the greenhouse early in the year, but remember to take them back in at night.

Feeding

Correct feeding is probably the most important aspect of all when growing structures of this size. Over-feeding will not be beneficial so it is essential that you should feed little and often. Throughout the first season a high nitrogen content feed should be used, and this can be supplemented by adding a slow release fertiliser such as Chempak Osmocote No. 8 to the compost. This feed is in pellet form and the fertiliser is released according to the temperature of the compost at the time, the higher the temperature the more feed released.

SHAPE TRAINING

Fans

If you wish to grow a good-sized fan for display and competition within a British Fuchsia Society show, the plant must be grown with a short solitary stem indicating that it is one plant. However, it is possible to get a better looking fan, with less risk of bareness at the base, if a multi-stemmed plant is grown – there will still be just one plant but there will be several growths from below ground level.

Three-stemmed Fan

This form is normally used to create a fan which is approximately four feet in height. Choose a good strong growing and free-flowering cultivar – Display, Border Queen or Phyllis would be good choices. Your strong rooted cuttings will be stopped after the first set of leaves has been formed – this will give you one pair of laterals. (Three-leaved cuttings are not recommended for this purpose.)

The two side growths from this first stop will be allowed to grow on without any check. The side growths from these two shoots are at first stopped at every two pairs of leaves. When the two main stems reach 2 feet (60cm), one of the side shoots growing inwards towards the base of the plant will be allowed to grow on unchecked to form a third main stem. It is easier to fill in the lower space using the two original stems and then fill in the top of the structure using the third – naturally, as the pair of branches grow away from each other a very wide gap is left towards the top.

The major problem now is of course the filling in of the

whole structure so that it looks like a fan – there is quite an art to the process of filling the empty spaces. You will need a strong support system from an early stage and all the laterals must be tied in very neatly. It will be a matter of choice as to whether you allow the side shoots to develop three, four or five pairs of leaves before stopping. The plant will grow quickly so regular feeding and attention to turning it so that it will be equally good on both sides is essential.

Do not let the plant flower in the first year but keep it growing fast. Regular potting on into the next size of pot plus some judicious pruning of the root system will encourage this strong upward growth. Our aim is to get a plant about four feet high and four feet wide. At the end of the season, when taking the plant back into the comfort of the greenhouse, trim each of the branches back to ripe wood. Most growers prefer to let their plants go into a semi-dormant state during the winter, where they remain in green leaf but produce no additional growth – at least by this method it is possible to tell the plants are still alive even though they look somewhat tired.

In the spring, with the additional warmth of the sun, the plants will return back to active growth. They should be removed from their pots, as much of the compost as possible removed, and then repotted into the smallest size of pot possible – which could be down as far as a 7 or 8 inch (18 or 20cm) pot. All the top growth needs to be sprayed several times a day with tepid water, to encourage all the buds hiding in the leaf axils to swell and to start growing. Throughout this second season continue to get good growth, filling in the structure so that it is a complete mass of foliage, turn it regularly in an endeavour to get depth of foliage at the rear, and keep potting on when the occasion arises. Regular feeding with a high nitrogen content feed at quarter strength will help to maintain the growth. By the end of the second and subsequent seasons, your plants will probably be in pots of 14 inches (35cm) in diameter. Ensure that your framework is strong and that any stakes or cross members which become weak are replaced.

During the second and subsequent seasons your plants can be allowed to flower. The timing of the flowering for show purposes will be the same as with bush-type growth and will depend upon the cultivar used. It is only when the plants are in full flower that you can really appreciate the worth of spending so much time in the training of these structures.

Four-stemmed Fan

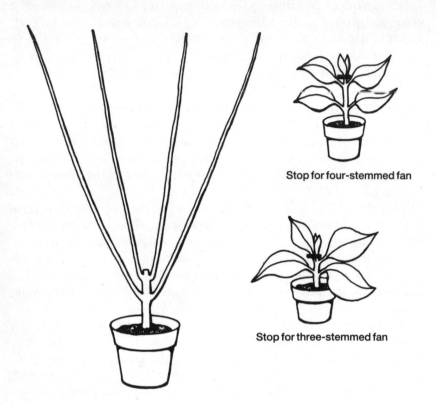

Stop for four-stemmed fan

Stop for three-stemmed fan

Four-stemmed Fan

This will finish off as a much larger structure than the one just described, so you must consider the amount of space available for growing and winter storage. The height to work towards is 6 feet (2m) or more with a spread of 4½ to 5 feet (1½m).

The rooted cutting is stopped after the second set of leaves. There will therefore be four subsequent growing points which will form the main structure. These four branches will be allowed to grow on unstopped until they reach the total height required. Good feeding and regular potting will be necessary to achieve this height. The side shoots on all of these branches will be allowed to form and will be stopped initially at each second pair of leaves. However, as with the previous shape, as the shoots develop higher up the stems it will be necessary to allow the side shoots to grow to a greater length in order for their foliage to fill in the ever-widening gap.

Again, take great care with the staking of this type of plant, placing the cross members at every three or four inches. Side shoots must be tied in carefully and judiciously to completely cover the structure. Again, the second year will see the fruits of your efforts.

Shrub-grown Fan

Although this shape is still grown from a single plant, as the rules stand at the moment it would not be acceptable to judges at a British Fuchsia Society show, as being shrub-trained it will have more than one growth coming from below compost level. Undoubtedly, though, a plant grown under this method will give great pleasure and will be beautiful to look at for eight to ten years.

Again a well-rooted cutting will be needed and this will be allowed to grow two pairs of leaves before being stopped, to produce four strong growing laterals which will be used as the main lead branches. Rapid growth is essential and this can only be achieved when there is root growth so it will be necessary to pot on as soon as roots are seen in the pot. When repotting do not place a great quantity of fresh compost in the base of the new pot but stand the old root ball on a thin layer, completely cover the root ball and fill the remainder of the pot with fresh compost. Your plant will gradually be potted lower and lower in the pots until the four branches are appearing from below the surface of the compost. You will find that roots will form from those submerged shoots thus increasing the root ball of the plant.

The laterals will be allowed to grow unchecked for three feet (1m), stopping the side shoots at each two pairs of leaves in the initial stages but allowing them to grow longer as the gap widens for filling. At 3 feet (1m), stop all four leads and train the top breaks of each so that you now have eight main stems. This increase in the number of growing shoots will of course help with the filling in of the upper parts of the structure. When the plant has reached a total of approximately 6 feet (2m) the same procedure can be adopted, pinching out the growing tips of the eight stems and encouraging the resultant sixteen shoots to continue their upward growth.

During the whole of this time, ensure that the pot does not completely fill with roots, potting on whenever necessary. By the end of the season the plants should be in 14–18 inch (36–46cm) pots. The higher the structure grows the more danger there is that it will become bare at the bottom. This is something that you should try to avoid so, if you are lucky enough to get fresh growth coming from below soil level, use this to fill in the base of the plant.

The design and the height of the framework upon which you build your plant will be a matter of personal choice. But bear in mind that such a large structure will need a very strong framework and will need, at the end of the season, to be brought in under cover. Also bear in mind that, having grown such a wonderful plant, you will wish to show it to as many people as possible and transportation could be quite a problem.

Espaliers

The basic shape of an espalier trained tree is a little difficult to describe. Fruit trees grown by this method have their major branches trained horizontally from the main trunk with side shoots growing perpendicularly from these. When dealing with a plant such as a fuchsia, using the same method of training, the finished effect will be very similar to that obtained by growing a fan. Both structures are viewed from the front but a fan has an overall width of approximately two-thirds of its height, whereas a completed espalier will have a far more semi-circular shape. There is not a great deal of difference really and it is understandable that some viewers will be confused.

There are two main types of espalier the first, a permanent structure, could grace a large conservatory and the second, a large structure, can be transported to shows if so desired.

The Conservatory Espalier

It is recommended that when you consider growing a plant of this type that a fairly large number of rooted cuttings should be available. There are bound to be a number of failures when the initial training programme starts. Your rooted cuttings need to be stopped after the first pair of leaves and the resultant two shoots should be allowed to grow as quickly and as lushly as possible. Growth is allowed to continue until five pairs of leaves have been formed on each stem. At this stage problems might appear. The two strong growing stems need to be bent down so that they are at right angles to the main stem and horizontal to the ground – lush growth is necessary so that there is sufficient flexibility in the branches.

Both of these lead stems, once they are gently but firmly held in position, are then stopped. The resultant shoots, and

Portable espalier

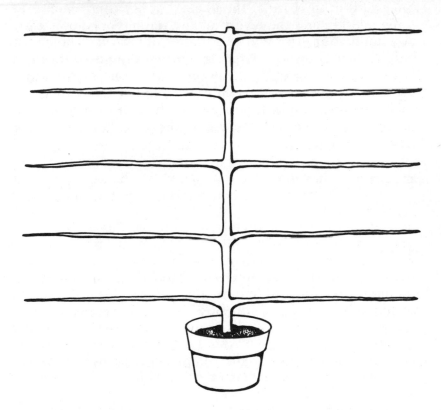

there could be ten on each side of the structure, will be trained in a perpendicular fashion and will now become the main stems used to form the eventual shape. These stems will be allowed to grow to the height that you require and any side shoots that form from them can be stopped at two or three pairs of leaves in an attempt to fill in the complete structure and finish with a wall of foliage and flowers.

Feed regularly during this growing process, and keep an eye on the amount of root growth in the pots. The final potting will be in a very large pot at the end of the first year and it might be considered necessary in subsequent years to plant directly into the greenhouse border.

The Portable Espalier
With this type, grow your initial cutting until five sets of leaves, plus the growing tip have been formed. The central main stem needs to be supported with a strong stake. The growing tip will be removed when these five pairs of leaves

have grown and the resulting laterals will be tied into a framework as near to the horizontal as possible. You will probably find that the top pair will need to be at a slight angle from the horizontal.

When the laterals have achieved five pairs of leaves they too need to be stopped and the subsequent growths from them will be stopped at every second set of leaves.

The overall shape will be similar to a half moon and can achieve a height of 6 feet (2m) with an outward spread of 8 feet (2½m). This structure is also viewed from the front only but regular training in the initial stages of growth will encourage a depth of branches and foliage which will enhance the overall picture on completion. Transportation, to put it mildly, will not be easy.

Pillars

There are two types of pillar that can be grown which are acceptable for competition in British Fuchsia Society shows – the first is a single plant structure and the second is a multi-plant structure. Both are reasonably easy to grow provided the normal rules of cultivation are carried out. The object again is to have fast growth in the first season, to achieve the height necessary for success.

Single Plant Structure

A good strong growing cultivar is necessary as a height of 6 feet (2m) is aimed for. Have some idea of your target height right from the start as your plant will be grown in two halves. The first half of the growth will be the basis for the foliage and flowers in the lower section and the second half of the growth will form the pillar for the upper section.

Your rooted cutting will be stopped after one set of leaves and the two laterals will be trained in an upward direction – I have called these two laterals A and B for the purposes of description. A will form the main stem which will eventually reach the maximum height. The side shoots from this stem will be removed until a height of three feet (1m) has been reached (this is similar to the process used for growing a standard stem). Thereafter the side shoots will be allowed to remain on the stem, pinching them out at each second pair of leaves, and the stem will be encouraged to grow up straight and true until the desired height of 6 feet (2m) is reached. Meanwhile, shoot B will have been allowed to grow naturally

Pillar

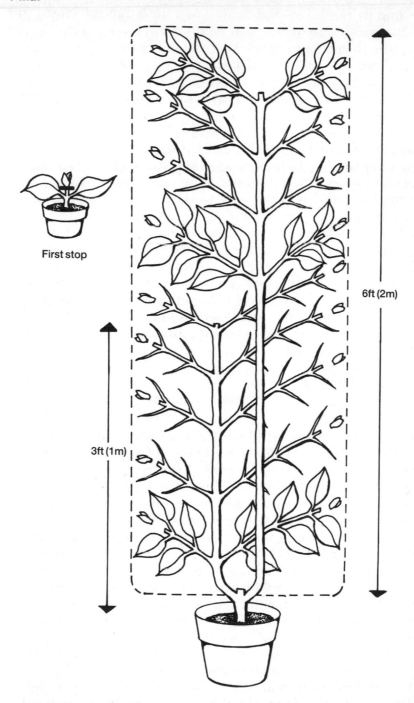

First stop

6ft (2m)

3ft (1m)

for the first 3 feet (1m) pinching out the side shoots at each second pair of leaves and then, when the height of 3 feet (1m) is attained its growing tip is removed.

From then onwards the structure will be treated as though it is just one main shoot. All side shoots will be stopped at each second pair of leaves and the object will be to get a pillar of foliage and flowers which is as wide at the top as it is at the bottom.

Single Plant (Alternative Method)

An alternative to the single plant method of growth as previously described would be quite simply to encourage each of the leading shoots to grow to the full height. This might well cause an overcrowding of the side shoots as they form and result in an imbalance of the overall structure. However, if, as the shoots grow upward, care is taken in the removal of alternate shoots from the stems, then this imbalance might be prevented. This will require some considerable attention to detail, but the side shoots on stem one will be removed at 1, 3, 5, 7, and the laterals on stem two will be removed at 2, 4, 6, 8 and so on. This method of training might well form a thicker and more even plant.

Three Plant Pillar

This is perhaps a slightly easier structure to grow and can be very satisfying indeed. You will require three cuttings of equal merit of the same cultivar – a good strong upright growing cultivar is essential. From the very first stage of potting, having rooted, they will be treated to all intents and purposes as one plant. When placed in their earliest pot, 3½ inches (9cm) would be recommended, a cane needs to be placed in the centre of them so that growth can be tied in and the stems grow straight and true. Each of the three plants will have a strong upward growing leader, and each will have a separate part to play in the production of this pillar – again I have labelled them for ease, as 1, 2 and 3. Number 1 will form the growth on the lower third of the pillar, number 2 will form the growth in the central third, and number 3 will form the growth on the top third.

Number 1 will grow upwards; all the side shoots will be allowed to grow but will be pinched out at every second pair of leaves. When a height of 2 feet (60cm) has been achieved by this stem (if an overall height of 6 feet (2m) is required) then the growing tip of shoot number 1 is removed.

Shoot number 2 will be allowed to grow strongly upwards but all the side shoots will be removed from it as they form until a height of 2 feet (60cm) is achieved. From this point onwards the side shoots will be allowed to develop, each being stopped when two pairs of leaves have been formed. When a height of 4 feet (1.2m) for the main stem of this shoot has been reached then the growing tip will be removed to stop any further upward growth.

Shoot number 3 will be encouraged to grow upwards as quickly as possible by removing all of the side shoots as they form until a height of 4 feet (1.2m) is achieved. This is the height at which shoot number 2 was stopped, so this third shoot will continue to grow upwards forming the upper third of the plant. From the 4 feet (1, 2m) mark until the final height of 6 feet (2m) is achieved, the side shoots will be allowed to develop and they too will be pinched out when two pairs of leaves have been formed.

With three plants growing in the same pot, considerable care and attention will have to be paid to the potting on process. As some considerable height is necessary for success the plants should not feel threatened at any time, or upward growth will cease and the production of flowers will commence.

Pyramids

The object when growing a pyramid is to try and achieve a Christmas tree shape. It is possible to grow this to be a good height of say 4–5 feet (1.2–1.6m) using a very strong, free branching type of cultivar. If such a cultivar is available it should be grown upwards without any stopping of the main stem but stopping each of the laterals as two pairs of leaves are formed. With patience the necessary shape can be achieved.

Single Plant Pyramid
Again a very strong upward growing type of cultivar is necessary. Your rooted cutting should be allowed to grow strongly until the third pair of leaves has been formed and then the growing tip should be removed. Allow the top set of laterals to grow sufficiently large that they can be handled without damage to either of them. Choose the stronger of the two laterals and remove the other one. The one that remains will now take over as the main stem and should be trained in an upward direction. When this new leader has formed three

Pyramid

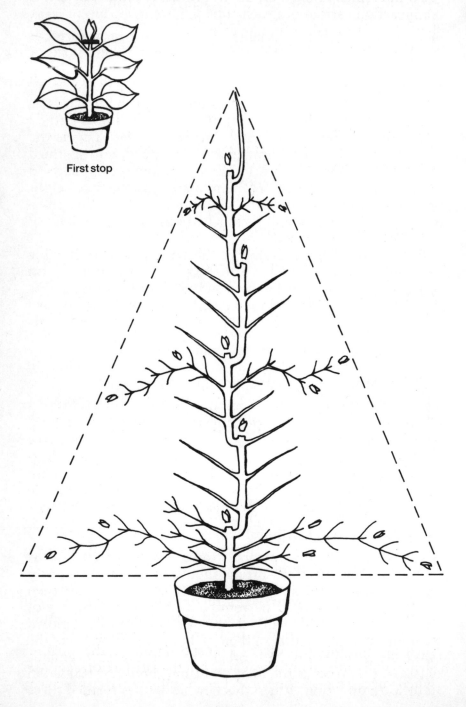

First stop

pairs of leaves then the growing tip will be removed again. From the resultant two shoots again select the stronger of the two and remove the other. So the process is continued and the same action carried out each time when three pairs of leaves have been formed on the leading stem.

All the laterals in the leaf axils of the whole plant should be allowed to grow, but each will be stopped at every second pair of leaves. The shoots on the lower branches will need to be stopped at an earlier time than some of those higher in the stem. The normal recommendation for stopping growing shoots of a plant is to remove all the growing tips on the plant at the same time. With this type of growth it will not be possible to do that in the first (growing) season as the different sections of the structure will be reaching that stage of maturity at different times.

Eventually, when the structure has reached its full height, and in subsequent years of growth, it will be necessary to treat the plant as a whole or else the flowering will be intermittent and not the full blaze of colour that you require.

Multi-plant Pyramids

The type of training using a number of plants will be very similar to that already described with the pillar. The first plant is used to build up the base, reaching a height of 2 feet (60cm); the second takes over the duties from 2 to 4 feet (60cm to 1.2m) and the third creates the upper part of the structure, from 4 to 6 feet (1.2 to 2m). The major concern is to shape the structure and ensure that the lower growths extend sufficiently far out to give the overall effect of a pyramid.

Conicals

The type of training for a conical is again very similar to that already described for a pyramid or pillar. The major difference is that the base of the conical will not be as wide as a pyramid. Care must be taken in the shaping of this structure once it has grown to its full height.

The major problem with large structure growing will naturally be the amount of space and time that they take up. Carefully consider the provision of winter care before embarking upon such an ambitious project. Transportation of the finished shapes will cause many a headache but the satisfaction achieved when successful on the show bench will amply compensate for this. Perhaps the growing of this type of plant might be better left to the few enthusiasts. It is important though that the way in which such structures can be grown should be recorded so that those who wish may attempt to acquire such skills.

Appendices

I FUCHSIA SOCIETIES

It is advisable when becoming very interested in a specific type of plant to become a member of one of the societies associated with it. Throughout the United Kingdom there are a great many fuchsia societies and it should be possible to find one quite close to you. These societies, many of which are also affiliated to societies specialising in flowers other than fuchsias, offer extremely good service and an opportunity to meet other individuals with similar interests. The British Fuchsia Society is of course the parent society in the United Kingdom and most local societies are affiliated to the BFS.

Most local societies hold regular meetings, usually with talks and lectures, and hold their own individual shows. Such societies have a moderate annual subscription and are well worth joining. Within their membership you will find those who are willing to pass on any knowledge that they may have acquired over the years. Space does not permit me to include a complete list of all the local affiliated societies and in any case details of the secretary and officers are likely to change. The addresses are normally obtainable from public libraries or the Secretary of the British Fuchsia Society.

Even for those who do not consider themselves to be expert growers of the fuchsia, it is an excellent idea to join the British Fuchsia Society, even if you do belong to a local affiliated society. Each member receives copies of the BFS publications, at present an annual and two bulletins, together with a copy of the constitution. Membership subscriptions paid before a date early in the year entitle the member to participate in a scheme for the free distribution of three rooted cuttings. The only payment requested for these is towards the cost of postage.

Membership also permits free admission to most of the shows organised by the society and also gives the right to exhibit free at these shows. Shows are held at present at the following centres around the country: London, Loughborough, Manchester, Bournemouth, Bristol, Harrogate, Swansea, and central Scotland. At the time of writing the Secretary of the British Fuchsia Society is Mr Ray Williams, 20 Brodawell, Llannon, Llanelli, Dyfed. All information concerning the Society can be obtained from him or the author at 11 Hungerford Drive, Reading, Berkshire, RG1 6JA.

The British Fuchsia Society was formed in 1938 and celebrated its golden jubilee with festivals, displays and shows around the country in 1988. The object of the society when formed in 1938 was to further an interest in the cultivation of fuchsias. Those aims still apply today.

The BFS has a membership in excess of six thousand and is by far the largest of the national societies associated with the fuchsia. There are however societies in most countries of the world which enjoy a temperate climate. The society which has taken on the responsibility for the international registration of fuchsias is the American Fuchsia Society.

II FUCHSIAS WORLD-WIDE

As will have been appreciated from the chapter on its history, the fuchsia is basically a native of the southern hemisphere. It has been a very welcome immigrant to those who live in the north and such has been the adaptability of the genus that we are able to produce and enjoy many marvellous variations of the fuchsia.

We are extremely lucky to be able to provide and enjoy the sort of climate which appears to benefit the fuchsia. It is when we consider the climates that others experience – greater heat or extremes of cold – that we begin to appreciate the efforts that some must put into the growing of their plants so that they can obtain such pleasure and satisfaction. During those occasional years when the sun shines seemingly endlessly from a cloudless sky, and local authorities entreat us to be careful in our use of water, we are able to appreciate some of the problems regularly faced by those growers living in much warmer climates.

We are certainly far more fortunate than growers of many other types of flowers in that we have a much longer season when the plants will be in bloom. It is possible to visit shows such as the Chelsea Flower Show, as early as the middle of May and have the pleasure of seeing fuchsias in all their glory. Granted the exhibitors at these shows are specialist growers but they do show that early flowering such as this is possible. For the person growing for the pleasure of producing good flowers it is possible with a minimum of effort to have plants in bloom during June and from then through until the end of the year. It should therefore be possible for any enthusiast to have the pleasure of seeing flowers over a period of six months.

For the real fuchsia enthusiast who wishes, whilst holidaying in other countries, to visit fuchsia shows or displays, a list of the societies of various countries follows. The addresses given are relevant at the time of printing and changes do occur. Fuchsia folk, being such friendly folk, will usually assist in any enquiry by passing on information or by pointing out the name and address of the current secretary.

American Fuchsia Society Hon. Secretary, American Fuchsia Society, 59 Aura Vista Avenue, Millbrae, California, U.S.A.

American National Fuchsia Society Hon. Secretary, 6121 Monero Drive, Rancho Palos Verdes, California 90274.

Australian Fuchsia Society Hon. Secretary, Australian Fuchsia Society, Box 97, PO Norwood, South Australia 5067, Australia.

Belgian Fuchsia Society Hon. Secretary, Les Amis du Fuchsia, Rue de l'Esperance 62, B 4000 Liège, Belgium.

British Columbian Fuchsia Society Hon. Secretary, B.C. Fuchsia Society, 2175, West 16th Avenue, Vancouver 9, British Columbia, Canada.

British Fuchsia Society Hon. Secretary, Mr Ray Williams, 20 Brodawell, Llannon, Llanelli, Dyfed.

Danish Fuchsia Club Hon. Secretary, Dansk Fuchsia Klub, V Merete Printz, Frugtparken 1, 2820 Gentofte, Denmark.

Dutch Fuchsia Society Hon. Secretary, Dutch Fuchsia Society, Floris V Straat 6, 4931, Geertruidenberg, The Netherlands.

Ethiopian Horticultural Society Hon. Secretary, Mrs. Fitzgerald, P.O. Box 1261, Addis Ababa, Ethiopia.

French Fuchsia Society Hon. Secretary, French Fuchsia Society, 26 Allée de la Prevoyance, Pavillions Sous Bois, France 933.

German Fuchsia Society Hon. Secretary, German Fuchsia Society, Pamkratiusstrasse 10, Grossforste 3208, Giesen, Germany.

New Zealand Fuchsia Society Hon. Secretary, New Zealand Fuchsia Society, P.O. Box 11 082, Ellerslie, Auckland 6, New Zealand.

South African Fuchsia Society, Hon. Secretary, South African Fuchsia Society, Mrs M.L. Copper, PO Box 1283, Pietermaritzberg, Natal.

Swedish Fuchsia Society Hon. Secretary, Agneta Westin, Ostermalmsgatan 68, S 114 50 Stockholm, Sweden.

West Germany Hon. Secretary, Deutches DG Gesselschaft, Ubierstrasse 30,5300, Bonn 2, West Germany.

Zimbabwe Fuchsia Society Hon. Secretary, Mrs Zeitsman, 66, Drew Road, PO Chisipite, Harare, Zimbabwe.

International Registration of Fuchsias American Fuchsia Society, Hall of Flowers, Garden Centre of San Francisco, 9th Avenue and Lincoln Way, San Francisco, California 94122.

III SUPPLIERS OF FUCHSIAS

The following list consists of nurseries who specialise in the growing of Fuchsias. It is not a complete list by any means but within it are those nurseries whom I can recommend from personal experience. It is possible to find many more nurseries advertised in the pages of gardening periodicals.

Arcadia Nurseries Brasscastle Lane, Nunthorpe, Middlesborough, Co. Cleveland, TS8 9EB.

B & H.M. Baker Bourne Brook Nurseries, Greenstead Green, Halstead, Essex.

J. Blythe Potash Nursery, Hawkwell, Hockley, Essex.

Goulding Fuchsias West View, Link Lane, Bentley, Nr. Ipswich, Suffolk.

Jackson's Nurseries Clifton Campville, Near Tamworth, Staffordshire.

Kathleen Muncaster Fuchsias 18 Field Lane, Morton, Gainsborough, Lincolnshire.

Littlebrook Fuchsias Ash Green Lane West, Ash Green, Nr. Aldershot, Hants, GU12 6HL.

C.S. Lockyer 'Lansbury', 70 Henfield Road, Coalpit Heath, Bristol, BS17 2UZ.

Oldbury Nurseries Brissenden Green, Bethersden, Ashford, Kent.

R.J. Pacey Strathern, Melton Mowbray, Leicestershire.

J.V. Porter   12 Hazel Grove, Southport.

J.E. Ridding   Fuchsiavale Nurseries, Stanklyn Lane, Summerfield, Nr. Kidderminster, Worcs.

Most of the nurseries mentioned offer a postal service, and all issue a catalogue describing the cultivars and species they have on offer. A stamped addressed envelope when asking for a catalogue will, I am sure, be appreciated. As with all things it is advisable to order as early as possible in any season. Stocks of certain varieties which are extremely popular rapidly become exhausted.

You can order the precise cultivars that you require from these nurseries. Most will offer to send substitutes, similar in appearance, if your choice is out of stock. The posting and packing of young plants is an expensive business and a charge is usually made to cover this but it is important that the packing should be of sufficient quality to ensure that your young plants reach you in as perfect a condition as possible.

When you receive plants, bear in mind that they will have been in the dark for at least a couple of days and will therefore have suffered a rather traumatic shock. It is advisable to unpack them as quickly as you can on receipt and place them in a warm but shaded spot. A lot will depend upon the way in which the plants have been packed. They may have been removed from their pots and wrapped individually in paper – the roots of these plants will be enclosed in the remnants of compost from their pots. Alternatively, the plants may still be in their own individual pots (usually 2 inch pots) and will therefore still be in their original compost. A third method is to send the plants in peat pots in which they were struck as cuttings, with the roots complete and possibly growing through their pots. Each of these methods of carriage will require its own treatment.

Plants sent using the first method will have received the greatest shock and will therefore require the most careful treatment. Gently remove the cuttings from the paper covering, ensuring that the compost around the roots is disturbed as little as possible. Also make sure that any label indicating the name of the cultivar is in place. If there is no label, merely a piece of paper, write a plastic label straight away – do not leave it until later. Deal with each one as an individual before proceeding to the next. Using your usual type of compost, place the plants in pots no larger than 2½ – 3 inches at this stage. Place a quantity of the compost in the pot, hold the plant in the centre of the pot with one hand and gently trickle fresh compost around the roots with the other. When the pot is full of compost and the plant is at roughly the same depth as it had been originally, give the pot a gentle tap on the bench to settle the compost around the plant. Do not firm the compost with your fingers in any way. Make sure the label is in position and then proceed to the next plant, placing the first one in a shady position. When the whole batch has been dealt with in this way, give a spraying overhead with clear water which has been standing in the greenhouse and so is at the same temperature. All the plants should now be placed in a humid spot in the greenhouse, shaded and given the opportunity to recover from the shock.

If you have a spare propagator into which the plants could be placed, so much the better, as they need to be given extra special treatment until they have become established. A daily, or twice daily, spraying overhead would be advantageous but do not water the compost until the roots have had a chance to start moving. As soon as the plants show signs of new vigour (the leaves will take on a firmer, glossier look), decide on the type of growth that you require from each plant. At this stage I take out a further insurance policy by removing the growing tips of each plant and using them as young cuttings. If by any chance the parent plant is lost I will then still have plants of the cultivar that I have chosen.

Plants which arrive in their original pots are likely to be looking quite fit and hearty although they too will need to recover from the trauma of being in the dark for a long period of time. They should be gently removed from the container and inspected to see what sort of condition they are in. Ensure that the label for each is still in position. I usually leave this type in their pots, but place them on a tray in a shaded place, giving them as humid an atmosphere as I can by spraying them once or twice a day with water from which the chill has been removed. Within a couple of days these plants should be looking much healthier.

I think it is important to transfer these plants into your own compost as quickly as possible and to repot them into pots which are of the same size as those in which they were growing. Remove a little of the compost and at the same time examine the root system – if there are any damaged roots then these should be removed with a sharp pair of scissors. Repot into your own compost, which should be just moist, allowing it to trickle around and between the roots. Again, do not firm the compost, but settle it around the roots by lightly tapping the pot on the bench. Continue with the daily spraying of these plants, keeping them shaded from hot sun, until it is obvious that they are growing well. Pot on thereafter according to the type of training you have in mind for each plant. Again it is a good idea to remove a growing tip, as a cutting, to ensure the continuation of the cultivar if an accident should occur.

Not many nurseries grow their young cuttings in peat pots, but if your cuttings arrive in this form, examine the peat pots carefully as you unpack them to see if there are any white roots showing through. If you try to remove the plant from the pot these roots will be damaged, so it is important to act carefully. A further examination will probably reveal that the peat pot is rather moist and it is important that it should be so. In spite of what has been said so far it is only fair to say that many growers dislike this type of pot and do all they can to remove the plant from it. I think this is a shame as, with a little care, the plants should suffer no setbacks at all from growing in these pots. The peat pot is designed so that roots will grow right through it, and the whole of the pot should be buried under the compost at the next potting on.

My advice for dealing with this type of plant is quite simple. Completely immerse each of the pots in water overnight so that they are completely saturated and soft before you start to work on them – in this condition they feel very soft and pliable. Using a pot sufficiently large (I would suggest a 3½ inch pot), completely bury the peat pot in fresh moist compost, so that no part of it is showing above the surface. Failure to do so will cause the upper lip of the peat pot to dry out and this will draw up moisture from below so that the whole pot will become harder and less pliable. Again make sure that the label for each of the plants is in position. The overhead spraying of these young plants will be supplemented on every other day with a good watering of the whole of the compost – I tend to keep this type of plant rather more moist so there is no risk of the roots being unable to grow through the peat pots. Again an insurance policy of a rooted tip is a good idea.

Hopefully, having taken care with your young plants, there will be no losses. In a couple of weeks your plants should be growing away very strongly and will have joined your main collection. It is strongly advisable not to introduce new plants to your main collection for at least a couple of weeks just in case an accident has occurred somewhere along the line and the new plants are carrying some type of disease which you would prefer to keep away from your other plants. A period of isolation will give any diseases the chance to reveal themselves.

IV GLOSSARY

Anther   The pollen bearing part of the stamen.
Axil   The angle formed by the junction of leaf and stem from which new shoots or flowers develop.
Berry   The fleshy fruit containing the seeds; the ovary after fertilisation.
Biennial   The term used for the process of growing a plant one year to flower the following year.
Bleeding   The loss of sap from a cut or damaged shoot of a plant.
Break   To branch or send out new growth from dormant wood.
Bud   Undeveloped shoot found in the axils of plants; also the developing flower.
Callus   The scab formed during the healing process of a cut surface. It also forms at the end of a cutting before rooting commences.
Calyx   The sepals and tube together; the outer part of the flower.
Cambium   A layer of activity; dividing cells around the xylem or wood.
Chromosomes   Thread-like bodies consisting of a series of different genes arranged in linear fashion. They occur in the nucleus of every plant cell.
Clear stem   The amount of stem free of all growth. It is measured from the soil level to the first branch or leaf. It is of importance when growing standards or bushes.
Compost   A mixture of ingredients specially prepared for the growing of cuttings, plants or the sowing of seed.
Cordate   Heart-shaped.
Corolla   The collective term for the petals; the inner part of the flower.
Cultivar   A cultivated variety; a cross between two hybrids or species and a hybrid. Normally written cv.

Cutting   A piece from a plant encouraged to form roots and thus produce a new plant. This is vegetative reproduction and plants produced by this method are true to the parental type.

Cyme   An inflorescence where the central flower opens first as in *F. arborescens*.

Damp down   Raising the humidity of the atmosphere in the greenhouse by spraying plants, benches or paths with water.

Damping off   The collapse and possible death of cuttings or seedlings usually due to attack at ground level by soil-borne fungi.

Double   A fuchsia with eight or more petals.

Emasculation   The process of removing immature stamens from a host plant to prevent self pollination, during the cross pollination of two plants.

Feeding   Applying additional plant nutrients to the compost in an effort to enhance growth or remedy compost deficiencies.

Fertilisation   The union of male and female cells.

Fibrous roots   Thin white roots produced from the main fleshy roots vital for the taking up of water and nutrients essential for healthy growth.

Filament   The stalk of the stamen.

Final stop   The last removal of the growing tip which a plant receives before being allowed to grow to flowering stage.

First stop   The removal of the growing tip of a rooted cutting to encourage branching into the required shape.

Hybrid   A cross between two species.

Hypanthium   The correct term for the tube.

Internode   The portion of stem between two nodes. Rooting from this section is described as internodal.

Lanceolate   Lance, or spear shaped.

Mutation   Departure from the normal parent type, or sport.

NAS   The abbreviation used by show judges to indicate that an entry in a class is not according to schedule. Exhibits so marked cannot be considered for an award within the show.

Node   Part of the stem from which a leaf or a bud arises. When taking cuttings, roots form most readily from this point.

Nutrients   The food used by the plant from the growing medium necessary for sustaining healthy growth.

Ornamental   A term used to describe those plants which have decorative foliage. The foliage can be variegated or of a colour other than the usual green.

Ovary   The part containing the ovules which, after fertilisation swells and encloses the seeds.

Over-wintering   The storage of plants during the resting period, the winter months, so that the tissue remains alive though dormant.

Ovate   Egg-shaped.

Pedicel   The flower stalk.

Petal   A division of the corolla.

Petaloid   Normally used to describe the smaller outer petals of the corolla.

Petiole   The leaf stalk.

Photosynthesis   The process carried out by the plant in the manufacture of plant food from water and carbon dioxide, using the energy absorbed by chlorophyll from sunlight.

Pinch   To remove the growing tips.

Pistil   The female part of the flower, consisting of the ovary, stigma and style.

Pot bound   When the plant container is full of roots to such an extent that the plant will become starved of nutrients.

Pot on   To transfer the plant from one size of pot to a larger one so that there will be a continuous supply of nutrients.

Potting up   Transferring a seedling or rooted cutting from its initial seed box or propagator into a plant pot.

Propagation   Increasing of stock by means of seeds or by rooting cuttings.

Pruning   The shortening of laterals or roots to enhance the shape of the plant or remove damaged portions.

Raceme   A flower-cluster with the separate flowers attached by short equal stalks at equal distances along a central stem.

Rubbing out   The removal of unwanted side growths, for example on a standard stem, usually in early bud stage.

Self pollination   The transference of pollen from anther to stigma of the same flower or another flower on the same plant.

Semi-double   A fuchsia with five, six or seven petals.

Sepals   The outermost part of the flower; four sepals and the tube form the calyx.

Shading   The exclusion of some of the rays of the sun by the use of blinds, netting or a glass colourant.

Shaping   To grow a plant into a definite shape by means of training the laterals or by selective pinching out of the growing tips.

Siblings   Offspring of the same female and male parents.

Single   A fuchsia with only four petals.

Sport   A shoot differing in character from the typical growth of the parent plant, often giving rise to a new cultivar, which must be propagated vegetatively.

Stamen   The male part of the flower comprising the filament and anther.

Stigma   The part of the pistil to which the pollen grain adheres.

Stop   To remove the growing tip.

Striking a cutting   The insertion of a prepared cutting into a suitable rooting compost.

Style   The stalk carrying the stigma.

Systemics   Insecticides or fungicides taken up by the roots and carried into the sap of a plant, thus causing it to become poisonous to sucking insects or protected from the attack of viruses. Can also be absorbed through the foliage if applied in spray form.

Trace elements   Nutrients required by a plant to maintain steady and healthy growth (boron, copper, manganese, molybdenum and zinc).

Tube   The elongated part of the calyx, correctly called the hypathium.

Turgid   The condition of the plant cells after absorption of water to full capacity.

Turning   The term used to describe the turning of a plant daily in an effort to achieve balanced growth from all directions.

Variety   Botanically a variant of the species, but formerly used to denote what is now commonly called a cultivar.

Virus   An agent causing systemic disease too small to be seen other than with powerful microscopes, but transmitted very easily.

Whip   A term given to a single stem of a plant being grown with a view to producing a standard.

Wilt   Drooping caused by a lack of moisture within the plant. Can also be caused by disease or toxins.

V BIBLIOGRAPHY

Bartlett, George   *Fuchsias – For House and Garden* (Crowood 1990).

Boullemier, L.B.   *Fascinating Fuchsias* (privately published 1974). *Growing and Showing Fuchsias* (David and Charles 1985). *The Checklist of Species, Hybrids and Cultivars of the Genus Fuchsia* (Blandford Press 1985).

Cooper, Adrian   Various   Fuchsia   Booklets   (privately published).

Dale Alan D.   *An Illustrated Guide to Growing Fuchsias* (Grange Publications).

Ewart, Ron.   *Fuchsia Lexicon* (Blandford Press 1982).

Goulding, E.J.   *Fuchsias* (Bartholomew 1973).

Jennings, K. & Miller, V.V.   *Growing Fuchsias* (Croom Helm 1979).

Proudley, B. & V.   *Fuchsias in Colour* (Blandford Press 1981).

Puttock, A.G. *Lovely Fuchsias* (John Gifford 1959). *Pelargoniums and Fuchsias* (Collingridge 1959).

Ridding, John   *Successful Fuchsia Growing* (privately published).

Saunders, Eileen   *Wagtails Books of Fuchsias* (Wagtails Publications).

Thorne, T.   *Fuchsias for all Purposes* (Collingridge 1959).

Toogood, Alan   *Practical Fuchsia Growing* (Crowood 1992).

Travis, J.   *Fuchsia Culture* (privately published).

Wells, G.   *Fuchsias* (Wisley Handbook No. 5, RHS 1976).

Witham-Fogg, H.G.   *Begonias and Fuchsias* (John Gifford 1958).

Wilson, S.J.   *Fuchsias* (Faber & Faber 1965).

Wood, W.P.   *A Fuchsia Survey* (Benn 1950).

Wright, J.O.   *Grow Healthy Fuchsias* (privately published).

General Index

Index of Species and Cultivars